Best Wishes
George Heiring

Gail Vail

The Seasonal Heart

Stories & Art in the Holiday Spirit

The Seasonal Heart

Stories & Art in the Holiday Spirit

Written by: George Heiring

Illustrated by: Gail Vail
special contributions by: Chris Ball, Shannon Candler, Cathy McIntire,
Ked Murray, David Siffert, Sherry Turner and Sandra Witty

Design: Michael Reinsch Design, Inc.

Published by: Gail Vail Creations
1361 Planters Trail
Greensboro, Georgia 30642
gvail@plantationcable.net

Forward

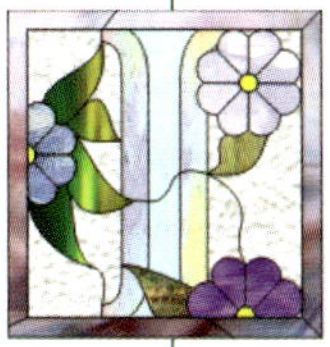

I first heard "The Crystal Promise," found on page 8, in my own home at a Christmas dinner party that my husband Jim and I hosted. As we gathered around the shimmering tree and shared the wonder of the season, George began to read the story of what actually happened one December evening in his small church basement in Illinois. The tiny congregation, he said, operated a shelter for the county homeless.

As George's cadenced voice filled the room, we realized we were in the presence of a master wordsmith. Our guests could feel the chilling cold of that Illinois December night. We could visualize "the street shepherds paying homage to the homeless baby." Our own warm, cozy room was hushed as George finished his tale.

"Oh!" I wiped away a tear. "George, you must publish your story!"

Fast forward…to my dear friend Gail who quietly and competently accomplishes things the rest of us only dream of being possible. I have long admired her artistic talent. In 2009, Gail single-handedly edited and published a gem of a book called "Seasons on Lake Oconee" which is filled with writings and paintings by talented residents of our Georgia lake community.

These two richly gifted people, George and Gail, have joined forces to give us a glorious celebration of the spirit of Christmas. Enjoy George's "The Crystal Promise" and all of his other holiday memories. Then take some time to linger over the nostalgic and moving illustrations by Gail and her artistic friends. You are in for a Christmas feast as you turn each page of "The Seasonal Heart."

Karen Hoven Fleece
Chautauqua Institute
Chautauqua, New York
Summer 2011

Dedication

Beginning in 1955, the year my wife and I were married, I began a tradition of writing a sentimental holiday story or poem for family and friends. Over the years, our list of encouraging readers grew as I traced the growth of our children and grandchildren, shared the sorrow of loved ones passing, conveyed the bittersweet of moving to new places, and recreated the sort of laughs and tears that are inevitably part of family Christmas.

This book captures those special memories, from the frustration of last minute toy assembly to the humility of homeless people seeking refuge in a church basement. My words are bracketed by paintings from some of the most talented artists in the Southeast. I hope "The Seasonal Heart" will help you rediscover the laughter and emotion that makes Christmas and winter months so special.

This book is dedicated to my wife Donna, my patient love and loving critic. I gratefully acknowledge the important role my grandkids play in these recollections as well as their parents, who remain as youthful as presented here.

Finally, I am honored to have my writings share these pages with the evocative art of Gail Vail and her fellow artists. Gail is both friend and editor, a publishing collaboration we honed previously on "Seasons on Lake Oconee" in 2009.

George Heiring

As a mode of expression, music and art need no translation. They are universal languages, each stimulating the senses in unique ways. For me, artistic expression is a need that must be fulfilled. It is my second language and I strive to find ways to evoke emotions through my paintings.

My parents always fostered my artistic growth and endeavors. While both had talent, neither had the opportunity to develop it. I dedicate this book to my mother, Marion Meisinger, and my late father, LeRoy Meisinger, who have been such great role models and a constant source of encouragement.

I have immense admiration for George and his remarkable gift of expression. I am delighted to collaborate with him on the colorful, visual part of "The Seasonal Heart." Rather than overtly illustrate each piece, I selected paintings that relate to the writings but can take you on a journey of their own. Also included are amazing paintings from seven of my artistic friends. I wish to thank **Chris Ball, Shannon Candler, Cathy McIntire, Ked Murray, David Siffert, Sherry Turner and Sandra Witty** for their beautiful artistic contributions to this book.

Gail Vail

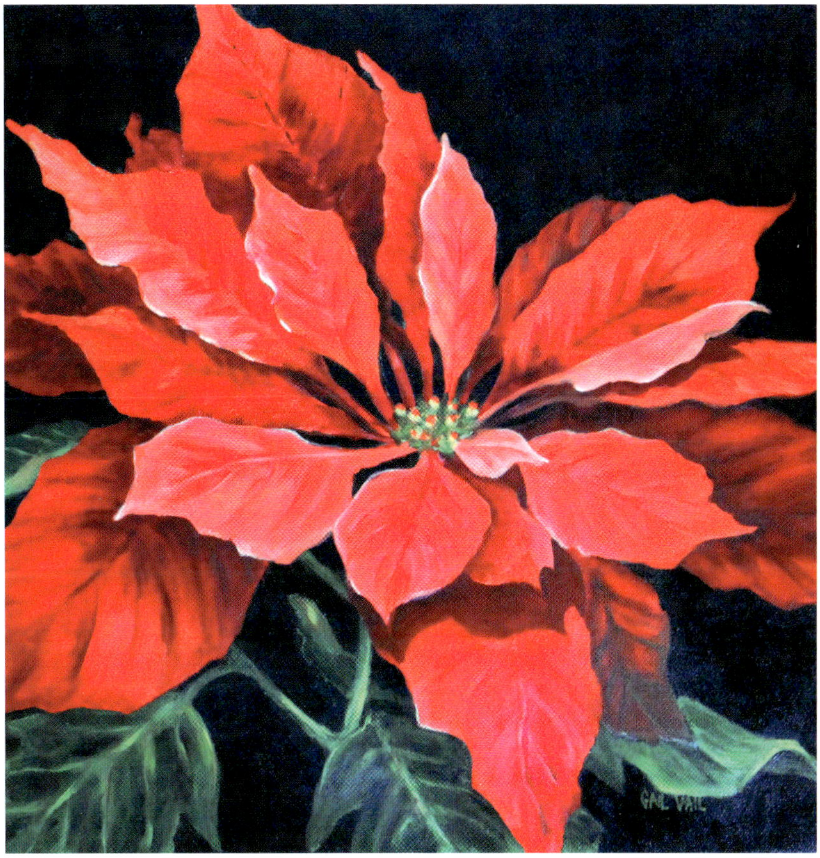

Gail Vail, Oil

Table of Contents

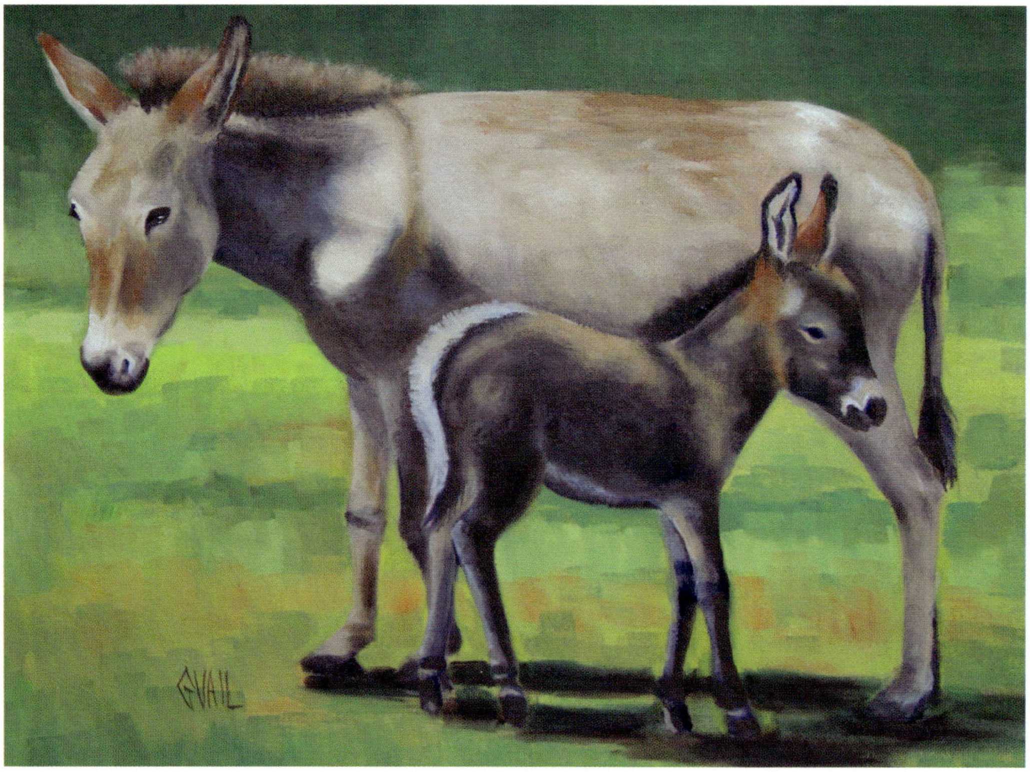

Gail Vail, Oil

The Great Nativity Riot

It started innocently enough. As usual, the decree went out from Caesar Augustus that all the world should be enrolled. That sent Joseph and Mary scurrying down the aisle of the church toward the cardboard stable. Mary placed her Cabbage Patch Doll in the manger, tucking the rag wrappings neatly into the straw to keep her baby warm. Joseph watched soberly, rubbing his nose and sniffing, for he was with cold.

At the rear of the sanctuary, preschool teachers, taking their cue from carols ringing from the choir loft, launched wave after wave of biblical hosts. "While Shepherds Watched Their Flocks By Night" put a half-dozen miniature shepherds in motion. Clutching crooked staffs twice their height, adorned in striped bathrobes topped by burnoose of pillow ticking and burlap, they came forward hesitantly, their parents video cameras and cell phones recording every precious step.

"Hark The Herald Angels Sing." Now came the seraphim and cherubim, resplendent in white sheets topped by wire-and-tinsel halos and packing wings ingeniously feathered with strips from plastic milk bottles. Over this fluttering host a battery-powered star of Bethlehem shown brightly, carried by the biggest angel using all the strength she could muster.

Thus the crowd at the stable grew. When the cue came for the wise men to arrive ("We Three Kings") it seemed uncomfortably clear there was no room for them at the manger. Nevertheless, the three pressed forward, intent on their historic mission to deliver the first Christmas presents.

In recounting the event, the phrase "pushy wise men" has been used, and that is probably unfair. But indisputably captured on eight different cameras is the video image of Balthazar coming in contact with an adoring shepherd, who stumbled backwards against a determined guardian angel. Sensing a threat to the sleeping babe, the angel retaliated with a push, sending the innocent shepherd reeling into a fellow herdsman armed with a crooked staff, which he abruptly lowered like a crossing gate to back off the magi. All three kings were dropped on their rumps, still holding tight to their gold and frankincense and myrrh.

Now it came to pass that others in this heavenly and earthly host were delighted to find this nativity stuff was not as boring as expected. So all entered into the fun by shoving the bathrobe or sheet next to them. Before Sunday school teachers could reach the fracas, the star of Bethlehem abruptly descended, its lights still gleaming as it cleaved the cardboard stable in two.

Mary, ever the divine role model, snatched up her doll and snarled at the mob, "get away from Jesus you guys." Joseph took up a defensive position behind her, sniffing harder and with greater menace.

Blessed are the peacemakers, for they shall quell riots in improbable ways. The peacemaker at this moment was three and a half years old. She had taken her angelic role quite seriously, allowing her mother to braid her blond hair, pin it to the top of her head and crown it with gold tinsel. However the tinsel was now askew over one eye. During the two-minute free-for-all she put her hands over her ears and yelled at intervals, "Stop it this incense!" No one paid attention until she pushed the volume up another notch. "Peace on birth!" she screamed, "PEACE ON BIRTH!"

The chaos stilled somewhat. Then the littlest angel began to sing "Away In The Manger" in her strongest voice, recalling the lyrics as best she could. "Way in da maingee no cupboard a bed," the tinsel haloed angel sang. Mary joined her in a voice now refined and gentle..."the little Lord Jesus"...as she warily put baby Jesus back in the straw. From the loft, the choir quickly found the harmony "...lay down his sweet head."

The music brought order to the nativity, probably because it is against the nature of small humans to slug a shepherd or bop an angel on the halo while a carol is being sung. "The stars in the sky, looked down where he lay..." The biggest angel hoisted the Star of Bethlehem over her head. "The little Lord Jesus, asleep on the hay." The wise men, their cotton beards dangling loosely, knelt, at last, before the manger.

Some in the church would just as soon forget the great nativity riot ever occurred while others enjoy replaying the videos to see how their kid fared in biblical combat. But there is a small miracle embedded in this event all parents seem to have missed---their kids were able to bring a foolish war to a quick, peaceful end with no help at all from the adults present. Adults, it seems, have yet to master "peace on birth."

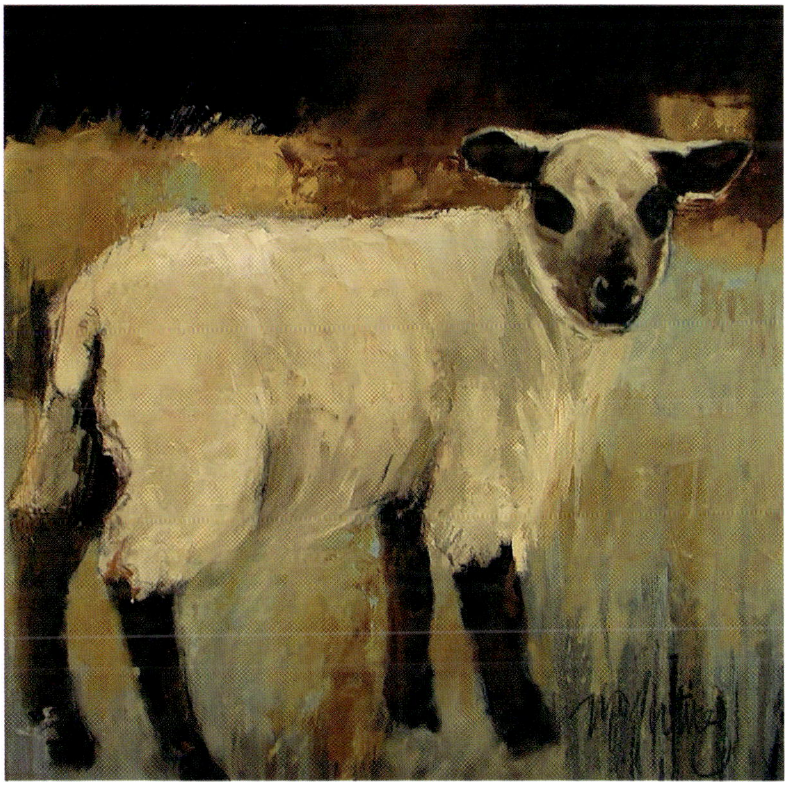

Cathy McIntire, Oil

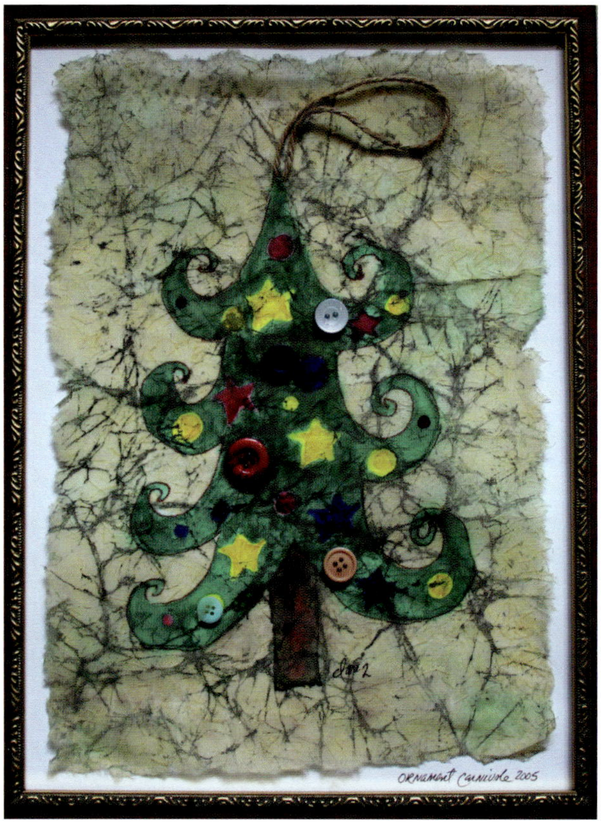

Sherry Turner, Batik

A Crystal Promise

On Wednesday nights our small church in northern Illinois fed and sheltered the county homeless. Once a month I volunteered to serve as overnight host, and on this night in mid December we were at full capacity. As temperatures fell into the teens, even those who usually favored solitary spaces in dark alleys were willing to settle for pads on the church basement floor.

Our twenty guests arrived by bus just before supper. They stripped off the layers of clothing insulating them from the cold and piled them guardedly on the mat they had chosen for the night. Next, a warm meal. Paper plates sagged under tuna casserole, jello salad, bread, and unsold pastry from local supermarkets. Christmas napkins were quickly snatched up for use as insulation against tomorrow's cold.

Simple as it was, the meal received expected, excessive flattery, especially from those who filled their plates a second time. Homage was paid to the fir tree in the corner adorned with paper ornaments created in the children's Sunday school. There were often boisterous arguments over the choice of late night TV programs, but on this night a pleasant, seasonal peace prevailed.

I felt good about helping on Wednesday nights. As jobs grew scarce and layoffs became more prevalent, the number of county homeless increased each week. Poverty is totally democratic, affecting men, women, old, and young. Sometimes families would show up with children, and that would give my heart a tighter twist.

But in the church basement there were strict limits to compassion. Our mission was to provide two meals, warm shelter and social order. Nothing more. We were cautioned not to slip our guests a dollar or two. Rules for guests were just as uncompromising. No one "stoned or under the influence" was admitted. "If any of you raise a ruckus," our site manager warned, "you're out! And once you're out, your not gettin' back in!" Our basement Eden, like the original, had a one-way door.

Washable sleeping mats were rowed across the asphalt tile, each fitted with clean sheets and worn blankets. By nine thirty, the carols on the kitchen radio were overwhelmed by hacking coughs and rasping snores. The air in the basement was laced with the odor of sweat, unintended urine and coffee frying in the server. A wind up alarm clock ticked relentlessly toward six thirty when the bus would return.

It was just after midnight when we received a call from a sheriff's deputy. A family of three had been found huddled for warmth in their truck. Did we have room? I glanced over the dark landscape of bodies on the floor. "Sorry, we're full up."

"They've got an infant with them," the deputy added quietly. Within a few minutes, my cohost and I found two patched mats in the furnace room and lined them against the wall of the hallway outside the main sleeping area. It was as close as we could come to a private room.

As we finished, a patrol car was sending bursts of strobe light whirling across the kitchen wall. Behind the patrol car was a pickup truck trailing clouds of vapor. Three dark figures emerged and moved toward the back door of the church, their shoulders hunched against the cold, their breath misting in the air. The deputy paused only long enough to say thanks, then retreated to his car. His mercy mission was completed, and his police radio was already crackling with new demands.

The lock on the door clicked shut. Our new guests stood for a moment in the shadows before the man stepped forward under the hallway light. Then I could see he was not a man at all but a boy in his late teens. His dark hair was stretched into a ponytail from which several strands had escaped. Beneath a skimpy growth of beard, his cheeks flushed pink from the cold. He wore a grimy nylon jacket, faded jeans, and black, muddy boots. He gripped a bag adorned with grinning teddy bears. His eyes were narrow with defiance.

"We made you a place over there," I said, gesturing toward the mats. "We tried to get you off by yourselves."

"We're not gonna sleep here. Not with street bums," he said bitterly. "We were doin' fine til the law came along. Jus' unlock the door and let us out. We'll sleep in the truck."

I nodded toward the figures lumped in the darkened dormitory. "Oh, they shouldn't bother you any. They're out for the night."

A voice issued from the shadows, soft and cautious. "We're kinda low on gas, Jamie." The boy looked at his companion for a moment, his face knotted in frustration. Then he set the bag down on the nearest mat.

"How about some warm food?" I asked.

"We're fine." Jamie snapped, staring at the mat with the torn blanket spread over it.

The girl stepped out of the shadows. Her arms tenderly circled a bundle of pale blue. The hood of her stadium coat cast a shadow over her face as she tightened her grip on the baby. She knelt to reach into the bag, extracted a bottle and brushed back the hood of her coat. Her face was thin, without make up or lipstick and her skin had the pale color of milk glass. Her close-cropped hair was a tangle of dark-at-the-roots blond. Probably sixteen, I thought. Seventeen at most. It was not a pretty face, but her ice blue eyes were unforgettable. Wide. Pleading. The eyes of innocence betrayed.

"Could ya warm this for baby?" She held the bottle up as she glanced timidly at Jamie.

Within ten minutes the bottle was warmed and in use. The girl sat on the mat wrapped in her coat, knees angled up, the formless bundle secure against her chest as the milk bubbles drained slowly away.

Her name was Beth. As she fed her baby, she rested her head against the basement wall and began to talk. "Jamie didn't eat nothin' today, makes him cranky." she said glancing at her husband punching buttons on the microwave in the kitchen. "We jus' grabbed some potato chips an' cokes from the house yesterday. An' some food for baby."

She spoke of "baby" as if it were a given name, as if the infant was a temporary gift that might be reclaimed at any time. "The house", I learned, was her mother's. It had been promised to Beth, but after her mother's death last year, her father claimed ownership. Jamie and Beth objected. There were "words," and yesterday afternoon the young family had been summarily evicted.

"My Dad jus' kicked us out. He was drinkin'. Otherwise…" Her words trailed away in search of a more hopeful conclusion. "We don't have nuthin' saved up," she said. Her thin finger traced the edge of the mat beneath her. "Jamie really hates this. But I don't mind it so much. Really." She dropped her head to hide the rush of tears. "I'm jus' glad Baby's inside an' warm."

Jamie stepped into the hallway, a mounded paper plate in his hand. "Beth, you want some of this tuna stuff? Or they got macaroni and cheese."

Beth got to her feet balancing Baby and the bottle. Without a heartbeat of hesitation, she placed the bundle in my arms. "Jus' let him finish his bottle while I eat." It was an instruction, not a request. So I leaned against the wall in the shadowed hallway and for fifteen minutes became the unlikely guardian of our littlest guest.

The wide eyes looking up at me over the bottle were pale and blue as his mother's, but without her desperation. They radiated curiosity. Trust. *Whoever is holding and feeding me must be a good person.* In the season set aside to honor another displaced infant, I wondered how things would go for this one. There was such promise in his eyes, clear and rainbow hued as fine crystal. And every bit as fragile.

The bottle was finished, and Baby's head lay on my shoulder, his eyes closed. As I had done often with my grandchildren, I patted his back softly and hummed "By Baby Bunting." Beth reached me at the second phrase, gently lifted the infant from me and cradled him in her arms. "…Daddy's gone a huntin'," she sang quietly, "to get a little rabbit skin…" She laid down on the mat, and curved her thin body around her sleeping son. "…to wrap our little baby in." She pulled the tattered blanket over them both, still humming softly. Jamie finished a glass of lemonade and stretched out on the adjacent mat, his head close to hers. I turned out the light in the hallway. In the half-light from the kitchen, I saw him reach out and touch the back of her hand. Their fingers linked as they lay in the darkness. Maybe…I thought…maybe Baby will be one of the lucky ones.

Before the alarm clock rang, my cohost and I had coffee ready and boxes of cereal and bottles of milk and juice on the kitchen counter. Our guests rose grumbling about the cold they would face. Like medieval warriors strapping on armor, they layered on flannel shirts, sweaters, and vests with quilted linings spilling out of gashes.

When they discovered a baby was among them, they formed in ragged ranks to pay their respects. "Gotta beautiful lil' baby there," a whiskered old man said as he bent to get a better look. "Real sweet" comforted a gravelly voiced woman wearing tinted glasses. "Never heard a peep from it last night," she added, though I was sure she could have slept through an earthquake. A towering black man stooped, reached into his coat pocket and held out a piece of wrapped candy for the infant. Beth took it with a timid smile.

The bus arrived, its horn bleating in the darkness. The last donuts were quickly swept up. The homeless wiggled their gloved fingers in goodbye as they passed by Baby. Sucking on his morning bottle, he watched them shuffle past, his eyes wide and curious.

By the time Baby's feeding was finished, Jamie had the pickup started and the heater was already going as we stood in the hallway. "Sorry we can't let you stay," I said. "If you want, I'll call around and make sure you have a place for tonight."

"We'll be OK," Jamie said. "I gotta be at work by eight thirty. Maybe my boss will give me an advance so we can get a motel." He put an arm around Beth and gave her shoulder a squeeze. "We'll be OK …won't we?" He thrust out a hand. "Appreciate everything."

Beth said nothing, but brushed her pale, moist cheek against mine. I opened the door and tugged the blanket over Baby's forehead, then the family moved quickly into the winter darkness that had brought them.

The sound of the truck engine had died away, but I was still thinking of Baby. His unblinking eyes were etched in my mind. I hoped my littlest guest could detect in my face the hope I had for his future. I had broken the host rules, of course. I knew no other way. They would soon discover the money in Beth's pocket. I prayed that Jamie would understand my selfish need to offer a bit of help.

Miles away, the homeless were already taking up their solitary spaces on the city streets, in doorways, alleys and mission halls. Their indigent life may be the result of unjust circumstance or the sagging job market or flaws in character. It didn't really matter. We share this earth with people who need our help. Every day. Every night. They'll not easily survive without it. And we will never be whole until we provide it.

Such is the promise we make ourselves every holiday season. It is a promise made of crystal. Fragile. Illuminating. But on this winter night it brought momentary light into a dark hallway. Street shepherds bowed in adoration. A homeless baby was honored. The miracle we call Christmas was reaffirmed.

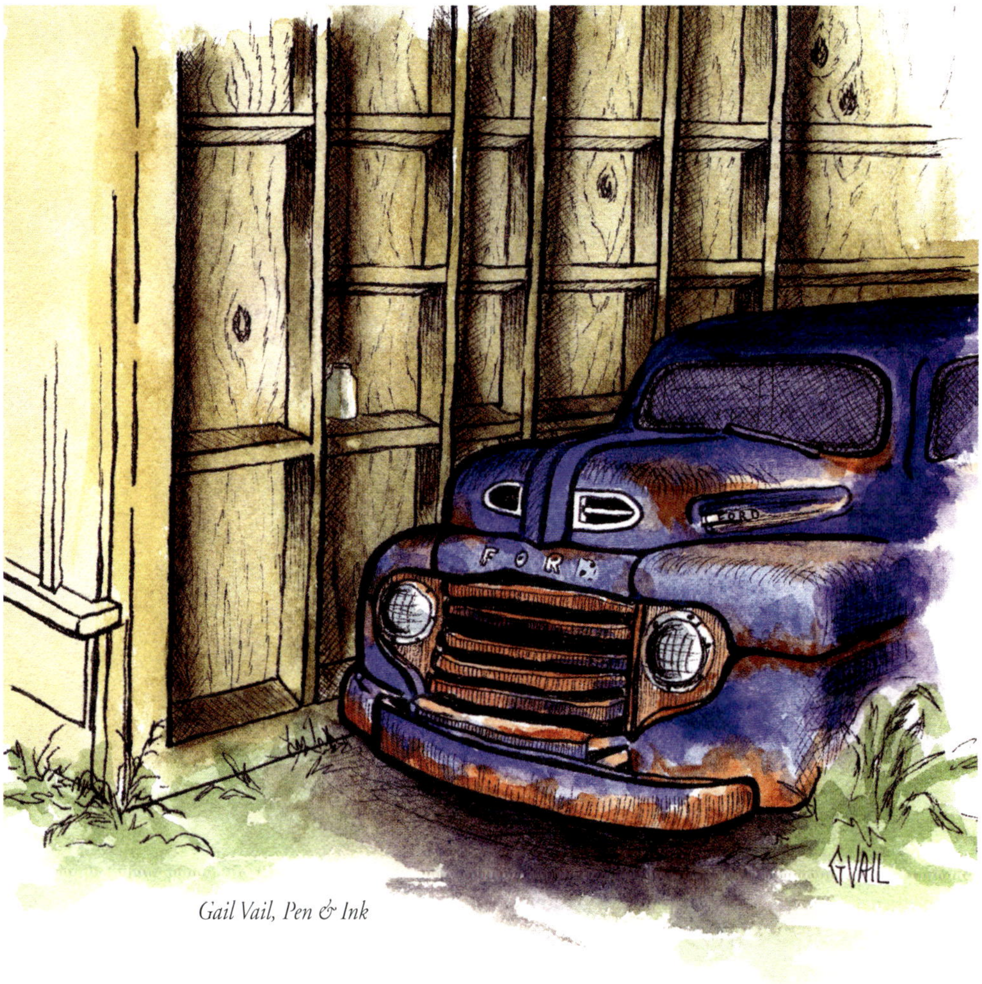

Gail Vail, Pen & Ink

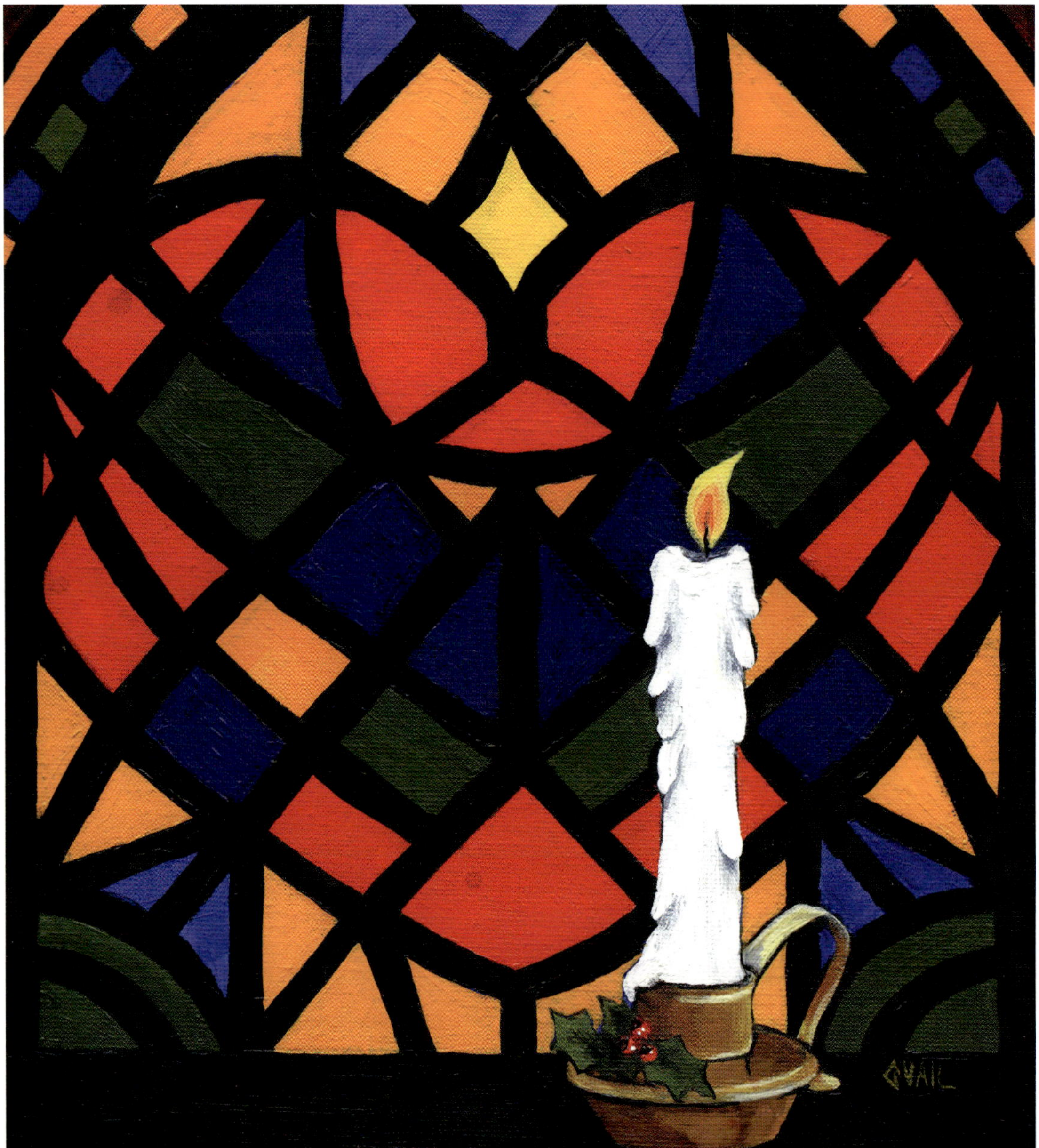

Gail Vail, Acrylic

Candles in the Window

Our church was the oldest in the county. A small, simple structure, on winter days its white clapboard bleached into the snow covered hillsides, enfolded in white land and sky. But when night came and light warped through hand-made window glass, the little church seemed fastened to the hill with golden buckles.

On Christmas Eve there were candles in every window. Though our pews were rarely full on Sundays, the ushers brought in fifty extra chairs for the candlelight service. Every one of them was filled. Carols pealed from the carillon in the steeple, familiar notes cast like seeds over farm fields and villages, rising and falling on the wind's caprice.

All were invited. As always, many came. The churchyard filled with cars, vans and pickup trucks just as it once did with buggies, buckboards and cutters. Mingled with familiar faces were those we didn't recognize. Children we had known brought children of their own. Families fragmented by distance or disposition were made whole again. Wanderers and seekers came to stay for one golden hour.

Our family filled one pew. From my place in the choir, I could see their faces in the tawny light. My two year old grandson moved along the pew from hug to hug to reach the aisle for a better view of the yellow star glowing in the Bethlehem window. When the choir rose for the first anthem, he imitated every movement of the director, an energetic maestro, swinging his arms up and down to mark the rhythm. On cue from the director, he raised a chubby finger to call for a crescendo, and when our voices swelled in response, he giggled with delight.

Once scripture was read and carols were sung, the passage of light began. Dancing flame moved from candle to candle, carefully tended by a universe of hands; hands veined with age...youthful and smooth...elegantly manicured...rough and calloused. Each offered its gift of light until all of us were golden in its glow. Then we sang. "Silent night, holy night, all is calm, all is bright."

"All bright," my grandson repeated, his wide eyes reflecting the fire in his father's hand.

The last chords faded. The service was over. Candles were snuffed out in silence, leaving a faint smell of smoke hanging in the sanctuary. My grandson gazed again at the tree laced with lights and red bows. He watched the choir file out. Then he reached to touch a smoldering candle, his eyes uplifted and imploring as he voiced a final request for all of us.

"More Christmas, please."

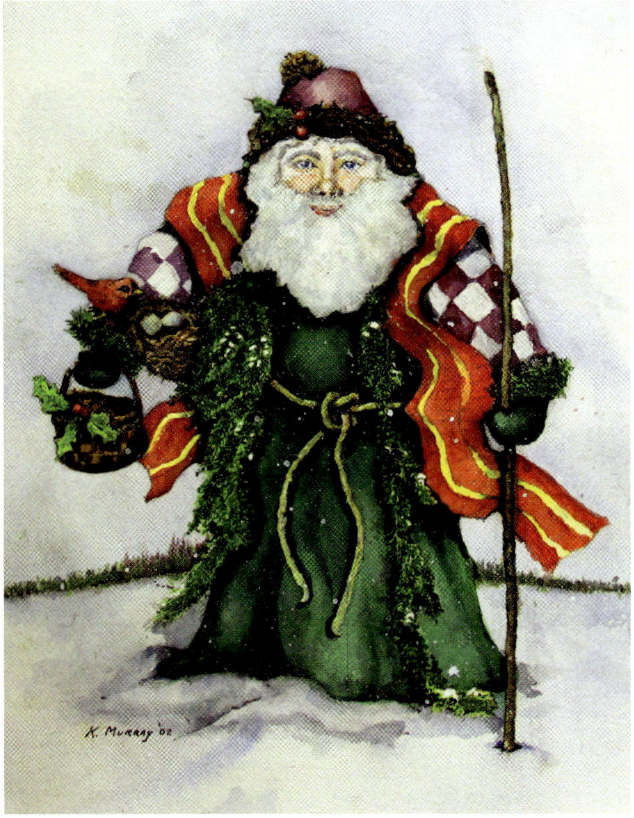

Ked Murray, Watercolor

Santa Watch

It was, after all, Minnesota, and four feet of snow in mid December came as no big surprise. But Daniel was from Georgia and unused to daily blizzards. Now, with the holidays approaching, Bing Crosby's constant crooning of White Christmas was a major irritation.

An Alpine landscape of eight-foot snow banks bordered the plowed streets close to Daniel's Minneapolis apartment. In order to see around the snow mountains piled up at intersections, he needed to bring his battered Ford pickup to a full, four-wheel stop, and that took some getting used to. Full stops at intersections never seemed necessary on the dry Georgia asphalt he was used to. What he never got used to was the ritual scraping of the windshield whenever his pickup stopped for half an hour.

He had moved "up north" barely one month ago. Before December blew in with a vengeance, he thought he might actually enjoy snow. He recalled the first greeting card-like dusting as it fell on firs spooled with Christmas lights. Then the wind picked up and drifts slithered across the paving. Carols booming from stores were drowned out by grating snowplows. Winter-wonderland lost all poetic appeal. Even his solar-powered watch had gone blank this morning--a final rebellion against sunless skies.

Well, tonight might be fun even if the weather wasn't. His cousin Ellen had coaxed him to play Santa Claus at her family Christmas Eve party. She delivered a large box with the required red coat and pants trimmed in fake fur, a wide black belt and black leggings. There was also a wig big enough to fit an NFL linebacker and a long, wavy white beard. The costume didn't feel convincing, and his conspicuous Southern accent wouldn't help. But he had promised Ellen and she was his only kin in this land of white excess.

By seven o'clock his Levi's and Georgia College sweatshirt were layered over by the baggy Santa suit and leggings. In preparation for his journey from the North Pole to suburban Minnetonka, he dropped his wallet, handkerchief, cell phone and his blank-faced solar watch into the pocket of the red jacket. Santa had to be ready for any emergency, especially since he was driving a 20-year-old beater with a poor heater.

Minutes after the baggy pants Santa reached the street and began hacking the ice from his pickup, the next Mid-western snowstorm materialized in a stinging blast that drove the first flakes across the street in horizontal stripes. *Man,* he wondered, how does *Santa stay warm and cheery in this kind of weather? Coming and going in fire-places probably helps.*

"Hey Santa, your reindeer on strike?" bellowed a wiseacre swerving around the pickup. Daniel stopped scrapping and responded with a blustering "Ho, ho, ho!"

Forty minutes later Ellen met him at the front door of her cheerily decorated Colonial. "You look terrific, Daniel. Everybody's back in the family room. Really appreciate your doing this. The little kids are so excited." She thrust a fat pillowcase at him to which jangling ribbons of sleigh bells were attached. "There's a small gift in here for each of the kids, all labeled." She gave him a quick once-over. "Ready to roll, Mr. Claus?"

"Lead me to the milk and cookies," Daniel mumbled, the fuzzy edge of the white beard sticking to his lips with every syllable. Jingling the sleigh bells and stamping his feet authoritatively, he followed Ellen into the din of the family room. "Ho, ho HO!" he offered in a forced baritone. "MERRY CHRISTMAS, YA'LL!"

The adults in the room responded with a welcoming cheer. Three teenagers exchanged glances with an "OMG" roll of their eyes. But the seven youngest children in the room were stunned into open-mouthed silence, trans-fixed by the man in red scheduled to arrive later tonight to fill their stockings and bring the toys they had yearned for. But this was way, way cool. Jolly ol' St. Nick was already here!

"The reindeer and I were doin' a test flight, so we thought we'd jus' drop down and see you kids while you were still awake." Daniel lowered himself into an empty easy chair. The furry pompom on his cap slid over one eye and he brushed it aside with a cautionary finger. "I know ya'll will be fast asleep when I come back later." Seven small heads offered nodding assurance.

"Good for you!" Santa said, untying the crimson cord securing the neck of the pillowcase. "I got a few little gifts for ya now. I'll bring the big stuff later tonight." He pulled a small package from the sack. "OK...this is a present for Justine..."

Within five minutes he dispensed small packages to everyone in the room. All had been shredded to reveal a va-riety of puzzles, small toys and candy. "Hey, there! Think I kin hear Rudolph up there pawing up on the roof, so I'd better git going." He stood up and jangled the bells on the depleted pillowcase. "Ya'll get a present, didya?"

A quavering voice responded faintly, "I dint." Santa looked down to see a sad-eyed four-year-old clutching his mother's leg. "I dint get a present, Santa."

"Oh my," Santa said with sincere alarm. "Let's see if there's one left in my pack for..."He looked up nervously at Ellen standing near the door. "There must be something in here for..." Ellen silently mouthed a name,"... for...ALEX. Are you Alex?"

The four-year-old nodded and stepped closer, peering optimistically into the pillowcase as Santa's sweating hand fished its bottom. Then Santa turned the case upside down and shook it. Nothing came out. The man in red glanced up at Alex, whose small lips were beginning to pucker in despair, and then he swung his gaze to Ellen, who was looking even more desperate than Alex. "Wait a second, Alex," Santa put a consoling hand on the little boy's shoulder, "it could be in my pocket."

His hand fumbled in the recesses of his red coat. Finally his fingers came to rest against the strap of his watch. His solar-powered, blank-faced watch.

"Well, now, here it is, Alex. Here's the special present I brought jus' for you!" He dangled the watch in front of the wide-eyed boy as if it were a diamond necklace. "My very own Santa watch. Tells time in every country I fly to. An' you know what? Sunlight gives it the power it needs to run."

"Awesome!" Alex announced excitedly, waving the timepiece over his head as the six other children looked on in envy. "I gotta Santa watch!" Then his brow furrowed as he confessed, "But I don' know how to tell time yet. What time does it say, Mom?"

As his mother lifted the watch from her son's hand her eyebrows elevated slightly. She peered at its blank face for a moment before brightening into a smile. "It's exactly forty two minutes after eight," she announced theatrically. Then she rested her hand on Santa's shoulder. "Thank you so much, Santa. It's a wonderful gift. Alex will learn to tell time much sooner now that he has his own watch."

"Jus' make sure it gets plenty a' sunlight to keep it powered up," Santa offered helpfully. "That's a problem up where I live." He gave Alex's mother an inconspicuous wink. "Oh, my…gettin' late. Time to fly back to the workshop and load up the sleigh." He rose, gathered up the jangling pillowcase, waved cheerfully to the children and started for the door. "Ho, ho, ho. Merry Christmas ya'll!"

As he arrived at the kitchen, his stride was suddenly interrupted by a pair of small arms locked around his knees. "I love you, Santa," Alex said holding on tightly. "I knew you wunt forget me."

"Alex, I'll never forget you. Never!" Alex's mother gently loosened the boy's grip from the baggy red pants. Santa stooped to look into Alex's bright brown eyes. "And when you look at yer watch, I hope you'll remember me."

Ellen escorted him to the foyer, checking over her shoulder to make sure they weren't followed. "That was pretty convincing for a southern boy," Ellen said. She lifted the long, wavy, white beard and planted a kiss on Daniel's cheek. "I wouldn't do any jewelry shopping until I come by to pick up the Santa stuff. I'll have a little gift for you. Something…a…timely."

Daniel opened the storm door and stepped into a world covered in four inches of fresh powder. A gust of wind pelted his cheeks with stinging snow. "Ho, ho, ho," he bellowed at the neighboring homes tastefully draped with strings of lights . "Merry Christmas to ya'll, and to ya'll a goodnight!"

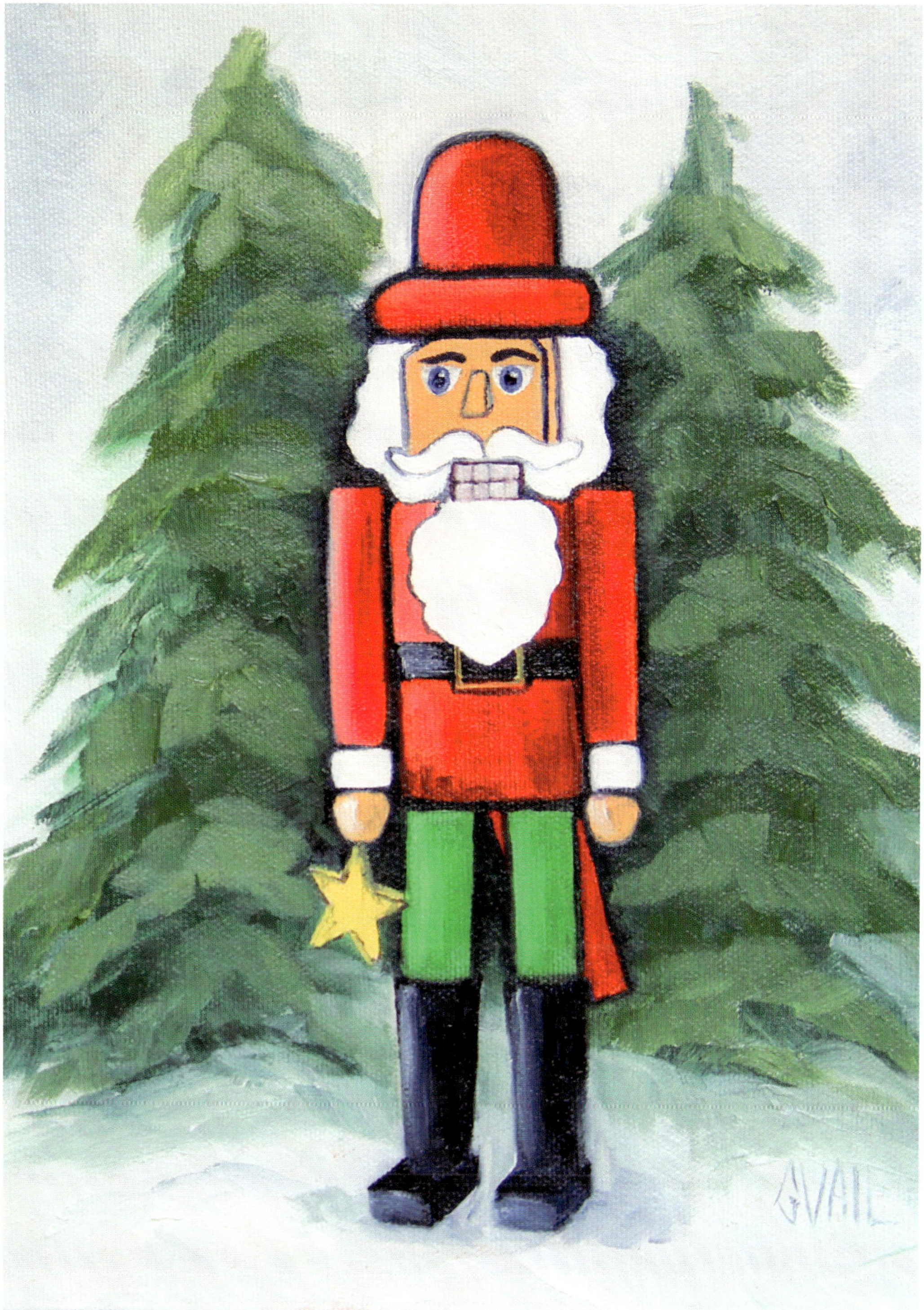

Gail Vail, Acrylic

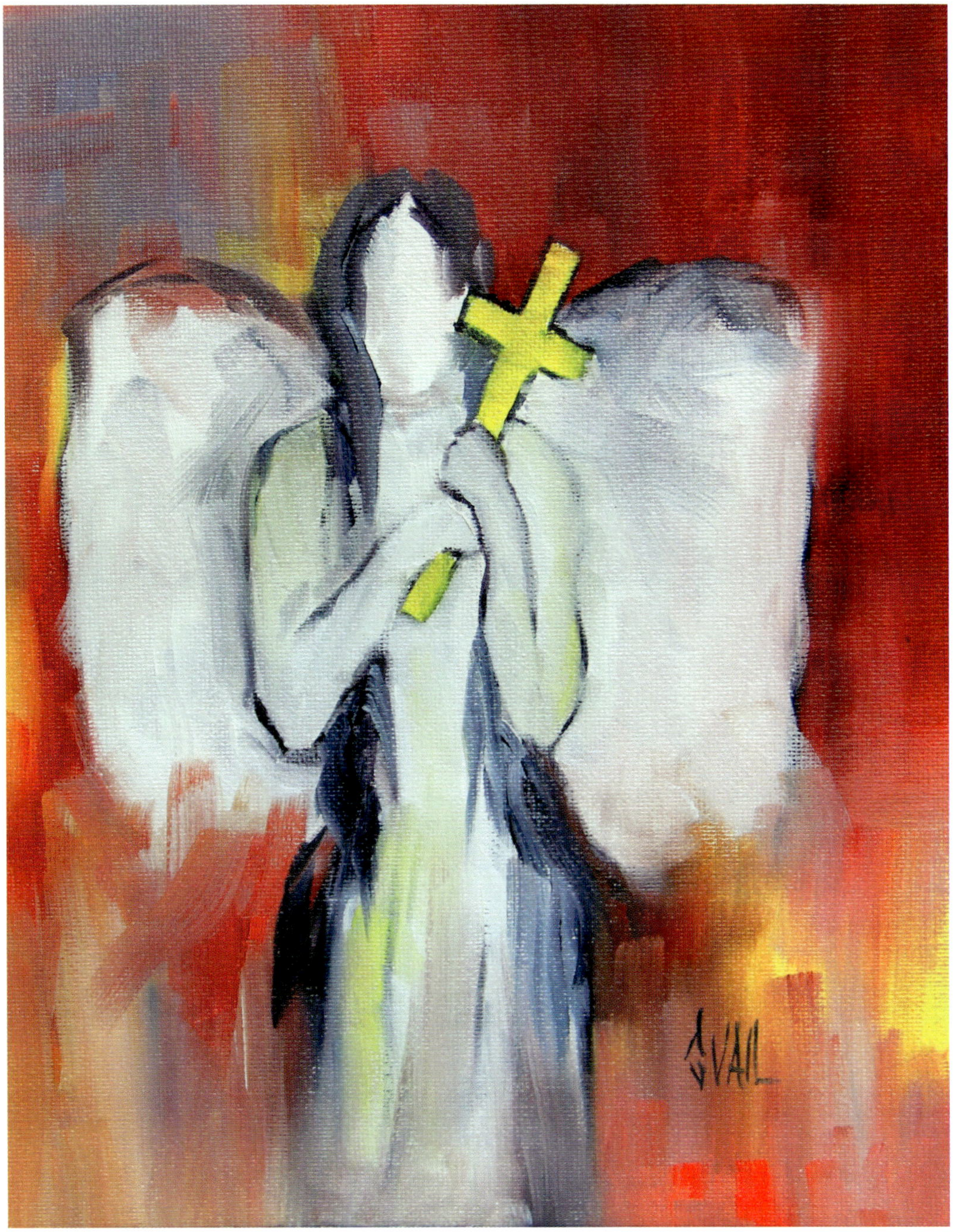

Gail Vail, Oil

The Cookie Contest

Kitchen windows cloud with steam
on Christmas Eve. Time to redeem
a drawer of jumbled baking molds.
Our Cookie Contest now unfolds.

Baked, pale cookies soon await
our family urge to decorate.
Frosting cups are given hue---
yellow, green, bright red and blue.

Subtler shades are quickly bred---
browns and blacks and purplish red.
But if colors used are not credible
the frosted sweet is rarely edible.

Contestants quickly claim the form
they're most inspired to adorn.
Sleighs and horses, giant boots,
angels, snowflakes, Santa suits,

Bells and stars and long neck geese
become each artist's masterpiece,
some flecked with tinted sugar grains
or candy beads or chocolate chains.

Pines are trimmed with silver dots
snowmen's buttons of red hots.
Our rules allow some alterations
to standard oven-baked creations.

A strawberry morphs to a baby chick
or a magi with crown just as quick.
Santa turns into a smiling fish
or a red fireplug as you wish.

Honors go to cookies "beautiful"
and those "creative." Less dutiful
artists receive the "ugly award"
if their creation is widely deplored.

To assure results are not distorted,
Contest judges are imported.
Unwary friends who come to call
referee this frosting free for all.

Losers are eaten without delay.
Winners are proudly on display,
our odd artistry expressed
in a gallery viewed by every guest.

A curious Contest, its real appeal
is what the cookies always reveal.
They may look good, bad or inspired.
Once chewing starts, they're all admired.

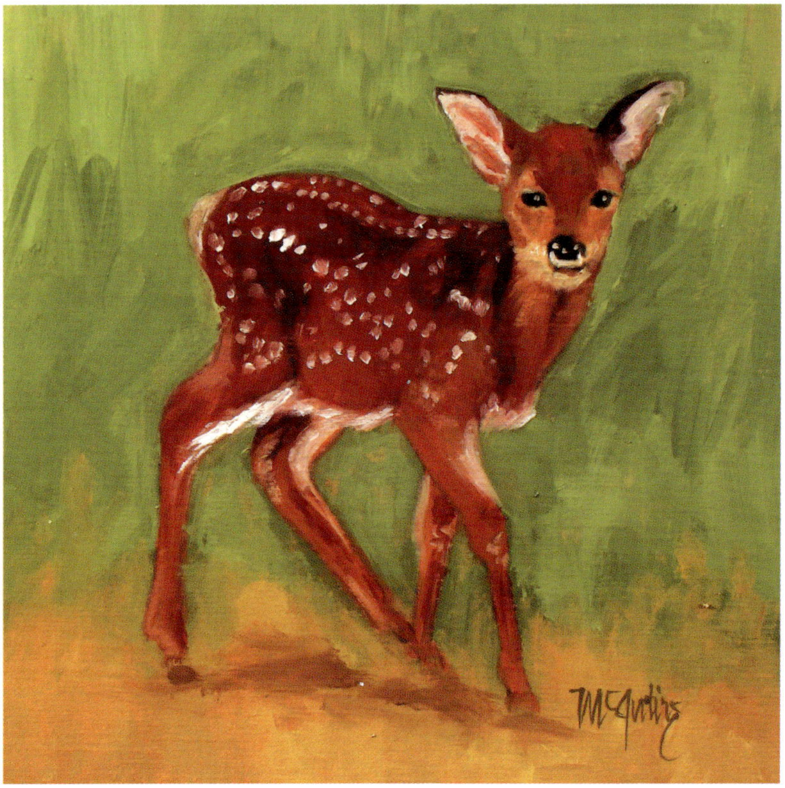

Cathy McIntire, Oil

A Home for Emily

Christmas was coming. Six-year-old Emily could see it coming. Strings of colored lights hung above the streets of the town. Store windows were full of toys. Christmas music was everywhere. Christmas trees shown brightly in windows of houses all over town.

But there was no Christmas tree at Emily's house. It was dark and empty. Her bed and toy box had been loaded into a big truck with the rest of the family's furniture piled around it. Now she climbed up in the cab of the family pickup truck, tucked her favorite pink scarf into her jacket and waved goodbye to her friends. Everyone seemed sad, and she was sad, too. She would miss her friends. She would miss sleeping in her room. She would miss playing in her yard. Most of all, she was sure she was going to miss Christmas.

"Why do we have to move?" She asked that question before, but she didn't like the answer.

"The business where Daddy worked closed down. He needs to find a job somewhere else," her mother told her.

"Why do we have to move now?" She asked again, hoping for a different response.

"We told you before, Emily. Another family bought our house," her father told her. "They want to move in before Christmas."

It didn't seem fair to Emily that another family would be having Christmas in her house while she was riding around in a truck. But she wasn't going to cry about it because that would only make her Mom and Dad feel worse.

So instead of feeling sad, they sang "Rudolph the Red Nosed Reindeer" and "Frosty the Snowman" as the truck bounced along country roads. Late in the afternoon just as snow was beginning to fall, the engine gave a loud "BANG". The old truck went slower... and slower...and slower. It inched to the top of a hill. Emily's Dad twisted hard on the steering wheel and turned into the parking lot of a small, white church.

Emily peered over the dashboard and saw a bus stopped next to the church. The people getting off the bus looked tired and wore ragged clothes. Some carried blankets. Most clutched small bags or paper sacks as they moved to the back door of the church.

Emily's dad raised the hood of the truck and black smoke rolled out. He frowned and reached for his toolbox. "Not good!" he said.

"Emily and I will wait in the church," her mother said. She held Emily's hand tightly as they left the truck and joined the line of people from the bus.

As soon as they entered the church, she knew she was going to like it. It wasn't the way it looked. The back door opened into the church basement. There were rows of mats on the floor and each mat was covered with a sheet. It was not a very pretty place. What was wonderful about it was the way it smelled.

"It smells like Christmas dinner," her mother said.

There was a large kitchen in one corner of the basement. Women wearing red and green aprons were busy cooking ham and potatoes and corn. Men with their sleeves rolled up were filling cups with hot cider and coffee and giving them to the people from the bus. A man wearing a red Santa cap with a little bell on the point stood by the door. "Merry Christmas and welcome," he said. "I'm Roger."

Emily's mother told Roger about the truck. "Bad night for a breakdown," he said. "It's supposed to snow for a while. But you were lucky to have your car trouble here. One night a week we provide shelter and meals for those without a home. Tonight we're serving our guests a special dinner to celebrate Christmas."

Emily wrinkled her nose and sniffed the good smell. "Well, Mr. Roger," she said, "We don't have a home."

Roger knelt beside Emily and the bell on his cap jingled. "In that case, we want you and your Mom and Dad to be our guests. We have plenty of food."

That sounded fine to Emily, but her mother looked as if she might cry. "We're happy to accept, but only if you let me help out," her mother said.

Half an hour later Emily's mother was working and laughing with the women in the kitchen. Emily's Dad came in from the cold and was given hot coffee by a gray haired man who asked him about the truck.

"I own a garage in town," the man said. "Maybe I can give you a hand." He found two flashlights and they went out to work on the truck before the snow got worse.

Emily wrapped her soft pink scarf around her neck and walked around the church basement, stepping carefully between rows of mats where the people from the bus would sleep. It was like walking down the streets of a small town. To Emily every mat was like a little house with a pillow and blanket waiting for bedtime. Roger said these people didn't have a real home. But tonight, each had a little house on the floor to move into.

One man opened a grocery sack, took out a clean shirt and put it on over the one he was wearing. A thin old woman took off her wet shoes and put them at the edge of her mat. Then she rubbed her feet and put on dry socks.

A big man with dark whiskers unfolded the bright blue blanket he was carrying and spread it carefully across the end of his mat. He leaned back against the wall, looked at the blanket and nodded with satisfaction.

When Emily sat down on the mat next to him, he frowned and scratched his whiskers without looking at her. "Is that your pad?" he asked.

"No" she answered in a small voice.

"Then, don't sit on it," he said. "That's somebody's home for tonight. That sack belongs to somebody from the bus," he pointed a thumb at a lumpy sack at the edge of the mat Emily sat on.

"Where's my home for tonight?" Emily asked.

The big man looked around the room and pointed to a mat in the corner. "Nobody's using that one." Then he reached down and smoothed the blue blanket once more.

Emily went to the mat in the corner. She pushed the pillow against the wall and unfolded the blanket, trying, as best should could to make it cover the sheet. But there were too many lumps and bumps. She was about to give up making her bed when the man with dark whiskers knelt on the floor next to her. His big hands spread her worn blanket out smoothly, tucking it under the edges of the mat. As he helped her, he said nothing. When her bed was made, Emily sat down on it and said proudly "Now this is my home."

Dinner was ready. The men and women in the kitchen piled food on each plate. Emily and her mom sat at a table with the people from the bus. They all seemed pleased to be with her and asked her about her school and her friends. Though many wore dirty clothes and some smelled bad, Emily liked talking to them.

The back door opened and Emily's Dad and the gray haired man came in. They stomped the snow off their feet and brushed it from their coats. "Good news," her dad said with a smile, "we got the pickup running."

The two men filled their plates and sat down at the table. "Your husband is very good at fixing trucks," the gray haired man told Emily's mother. Then he winked. "He's so good I offered him a job in my garage if he wants it."

Emily's dad smiled, "Sounds like it just might work out for us." He put his arm around Emily's mother. "I need to talk it over with my wife."

Roger took a shiny harmonica out of his pocket and played "Jingle Bells." The tiny bell on top of his Santa cap jingled as his head moved.

Everyone enjoyed the music except the big man with the dark whiskers, who sat by himself. He pulled the blue blanket over his shoulders and stared into space. Emily went to him and asked, "Is that blanket really extra special?"

"Without this blanket, nobody notices me. I'm just part of the street. But it's such a pretty thing. Comfortable. When I've got it around me it makes me feel special," he answered. " It's the only thing I own that's worth anything and I don't want nobody to steal it."

Emily clutched the ends of her soft pink scarf. "This makes me feel special, too. And it keeps me really warm."

He pointed his finger at her. "Then you hold on to it tight. Don't let yourself get cold or you might never get warm again." He pulled the edge of his blue blanket across his chest. "Folks without a home gotta look out for themselves. Nobody else cares much about you." He looked deeply into Emily's eyes, "Homeless folks got to help each other."

As Emily's mother and the ladies cleared away the dishes, Emily looked out the basement window. The storm had passed and the sky was decorated with stars. On the front lawn of the church she saw a small shed. Inside were figures of a woman and man kneeling by a box filled with straw. The scene had been dusted with fresh snow. When her mother came to the window beside her, Emily asked, "Is that the manger?"

"Yes," her mother said. "That's a crib like the one baby Jesus slept in when he was born. You can see his mother Mary and his father Joseph watching over him."

"Didn't they have a house to sleep in?"

"No," her mother said. "There was no house for them in Bethlehem. They stayed outside in a stable with sheep and donkeys."

"Were they cold?" Emily asked.

"Probably were, Emily. They were tired from a long trip. And nights there were cold. No one gave them a meal and a place to sleep like we found here."

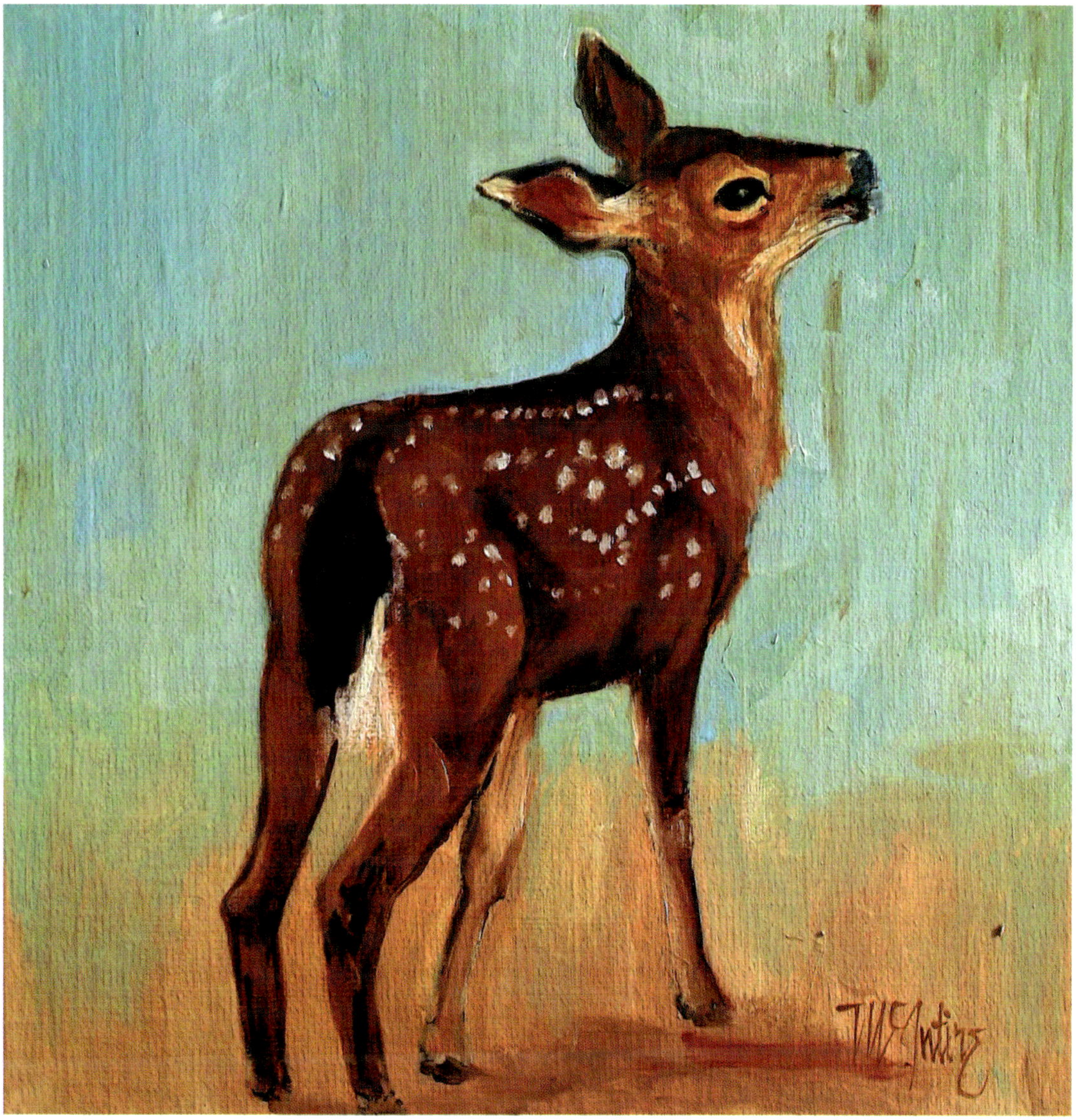

Cathy McIntire, Oil

After the dinner dishes were done and fresh cups of coffee and cider were poured, a woman from the kitchen played the piano. No one noticed as Emily pushed open the back door and walked out into the winter night. She tugged her pink scarf tight around her neck and trudged through the fresh snow toward the manger. She stood for a moment in front of the crib where a baby doll lay in the hay. Over the stable, a torn blanket of stars covered the sky. One seemed brighter than all the rest. Emily watched it shine above her, then brushed snow from Mary's head and shoulders as she listened to the music from the church.

Inside, Emily's Mother suddenly noticed she was missing. She looked for her in the basement, and when she couldn't find her, became worried. Roger and others checked behind the seats and around the alter in the church upstairs. Emily's Dad and the gray haired man put on their coats and searched the parking lot. But it was the big man with the dark whiskers who found her.

He found her in front of the snow-covered stable, quietly watching over Baby Jesus with Joseph and Mary. The big man noticed something else. Jesus's Mother now wore a soft pink scarf around her neck. Emily looked up at the big man. "You said people with no home should help each other."

The last Christmas music that night was played very softly on the harmonica. Before it was finished, Emily fell asleep on the floor mat she called "home."

Next morning the homeless people waved and climbed up the steps of the waiting bus. The big man with the whiskers stopped to say goodbye to Emily. It was the first time those on the bus had ever seen him smile.

"Time for us to get going, "Emily's mom told her as she put on her coat. "We need to start looking for a home. Your Dad has a new job."

Emily's Dad drove the truck out of the parking lot slowly so Emily could see if her favorite pink scarf was still keeping Mary warm. It was there. But something else had been added. Something extra, extra special, Emily thought. The baby doll in the crib had been brushed clean of snow, and now lay snug and warm under a bright blue blanket.

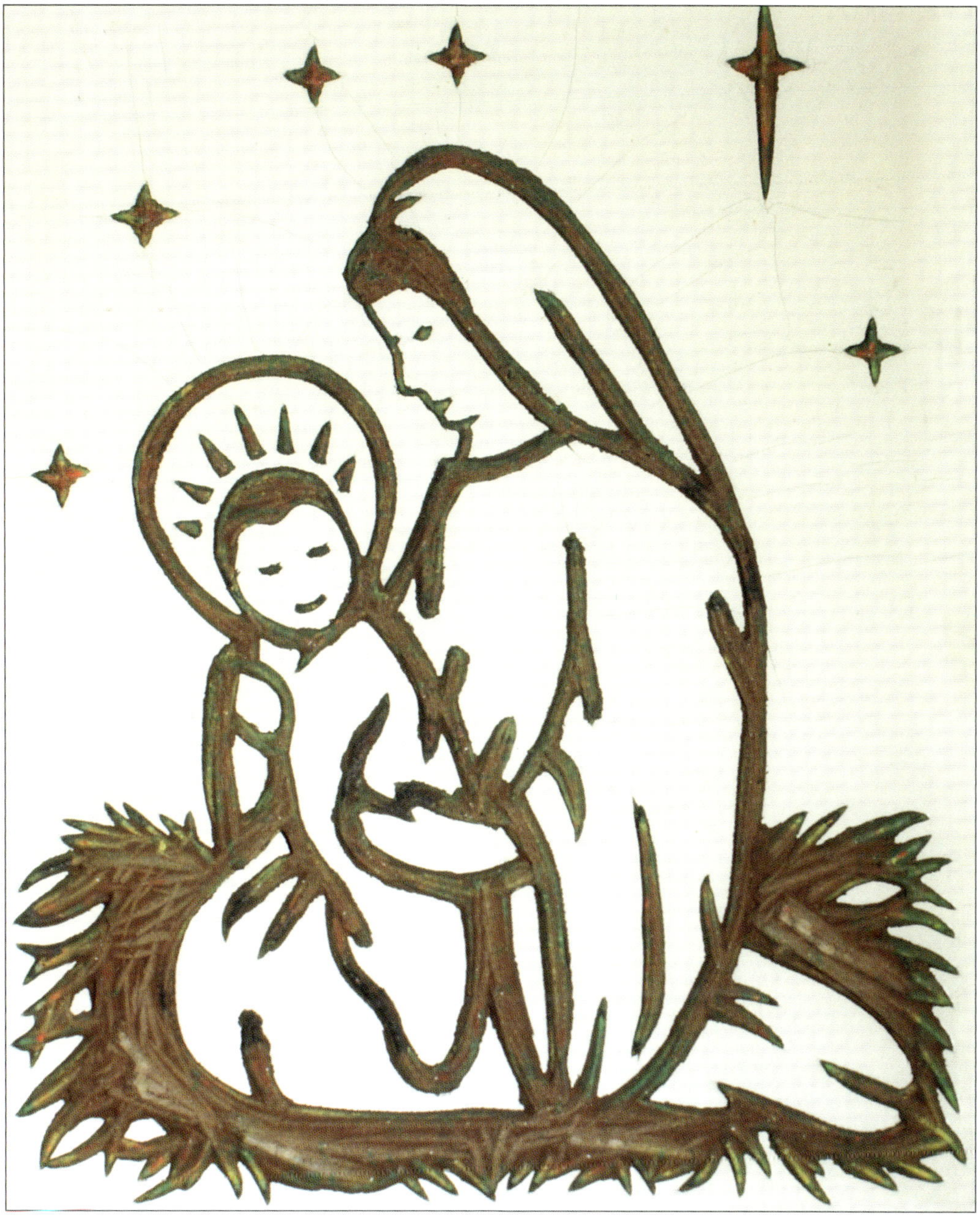

Gail Vail, Linoleum Block

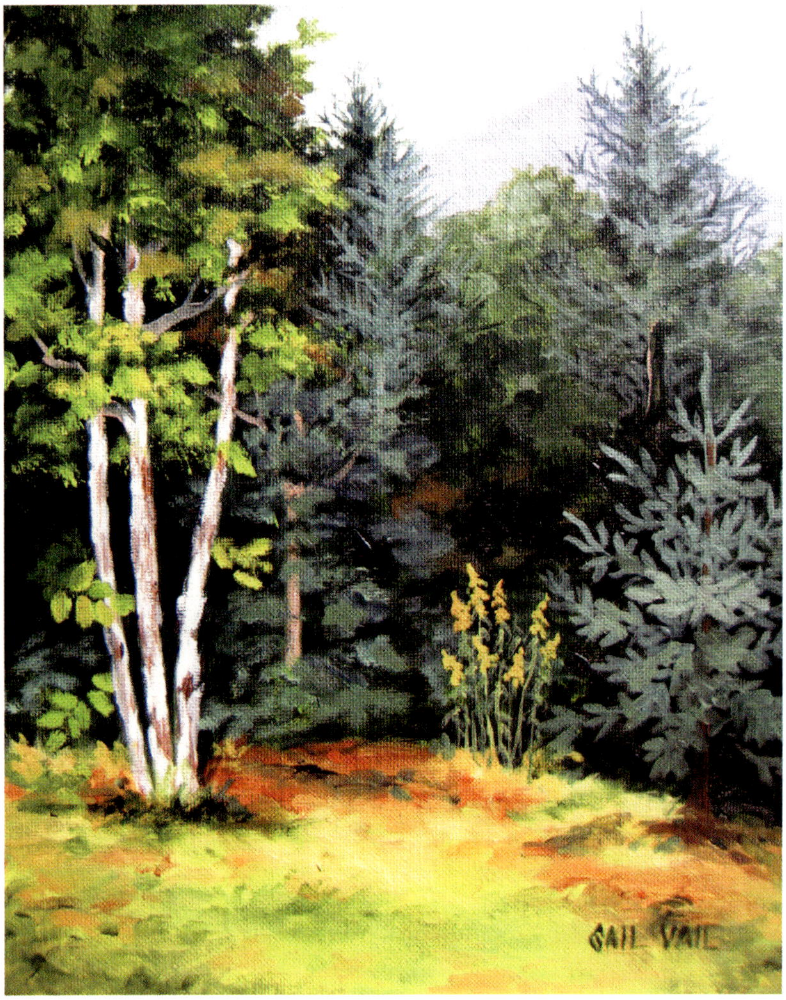

Gail Vail, Acrylic

Reconstruction of the Heart

Pine trees still surround us. A forest edges the lake in all directions. Tall, straight, their rough bark yields spindly branches with long-needle brushes that paint the Georgia sky with each fresh breeze. How different from the pine trees on our Illinois hilltop, their branches bowed low with the weight of snow, sweeping the ground like dutiful housewives.

We're gone from that Illinois hilltop now. One late September afternoon when oaks and maples we'd planted for each grandchild blushed scarlet and gold, the doors on the moving truck slammed shut and it groaned onto the road. Friends came to mourn, leaning against the front door as if to keep it from shutting on them forever. After awkward silences, they drifted away. The word "goodbye" was never spoken.

My wife and I went back in the house for one last look. We walked silently from room to room, arms wrapped round each other's shoulders, braced against a flood of memories. A quarter century of family spirits played about us in the late afternoon shadows. Our voices echoed in the empty rooms, mingling with conjured sounds of kids growing up, leaving, and bringing home babies of their own. Whispered lyrics of our life song.

Stripped of its finery and ambitious clutter, the house made its final plea. "How can you abandon me after all the years I've held you?" We didn't trust ourselves to answer. Tears spilled into the carpet, marking the turf with a stubborn finality as migrating creatures often do. Then we climbed in the car and drove away. In the mirror I watched our gate lamps recede until they were faint points of light in the darkening sky.

Our home is now in Georgia on a point of shoreline bordered by miles of brown water. It is already a home with a generous history, a bright and welcoming place where new memories have taken up residence. The laughter of seven grandchildren brought music to its rooms. Old friends have come long distances to share a glass of wine before the fire. Our second grandson took his first steps here. In her ninety-first year, my mother-in-law sat on the porch watching bluebirds nest and a Great Blue Heron glide majestically across our point.

The past is never really past. The heart is, after all, an elastic organ. When we think its contents have been neatly defined and cataloged, life gives us more to add. A transplant is rarely required. Just an occasional and loving reconstruction.

Quite often, after the sun has walked its shining path across the lake and evening haze settles on the water, I've seen gate lamps blink to life on the hill across the lake. Two small faint points of light transcending distance and time. Like stars in my private cosmos, they are beacons to the comfort of the past…and to the promise of the future.

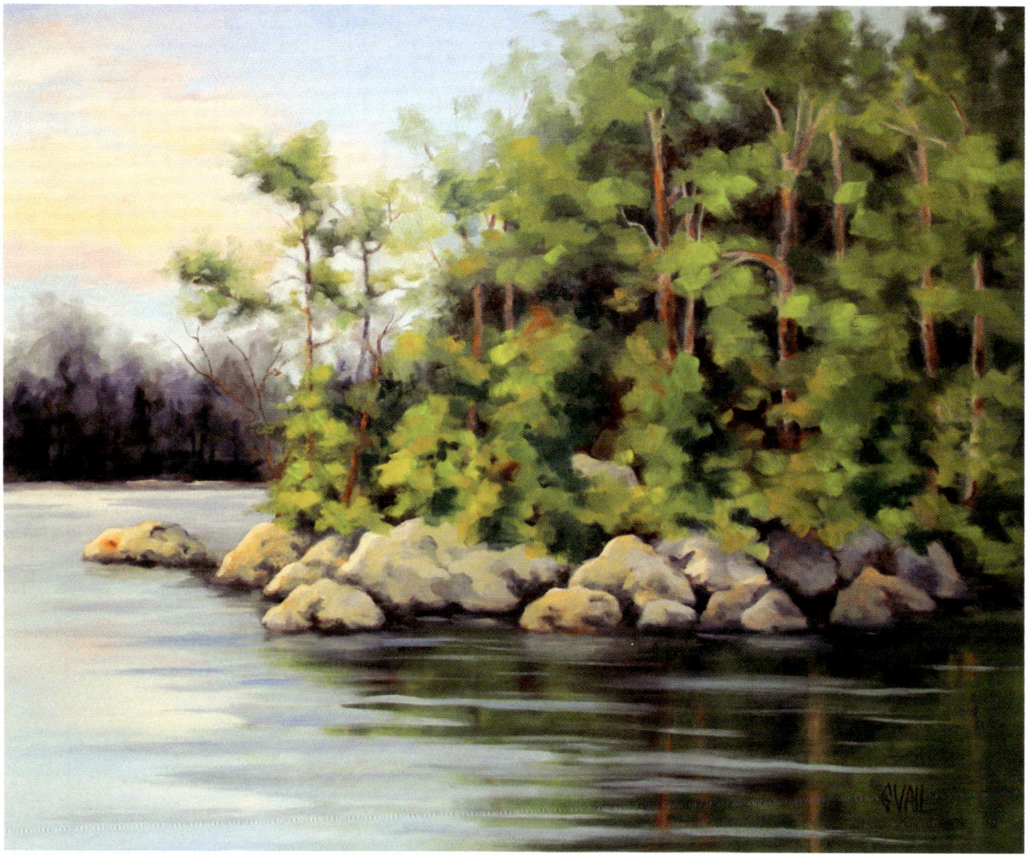

Gail Vail, Oil

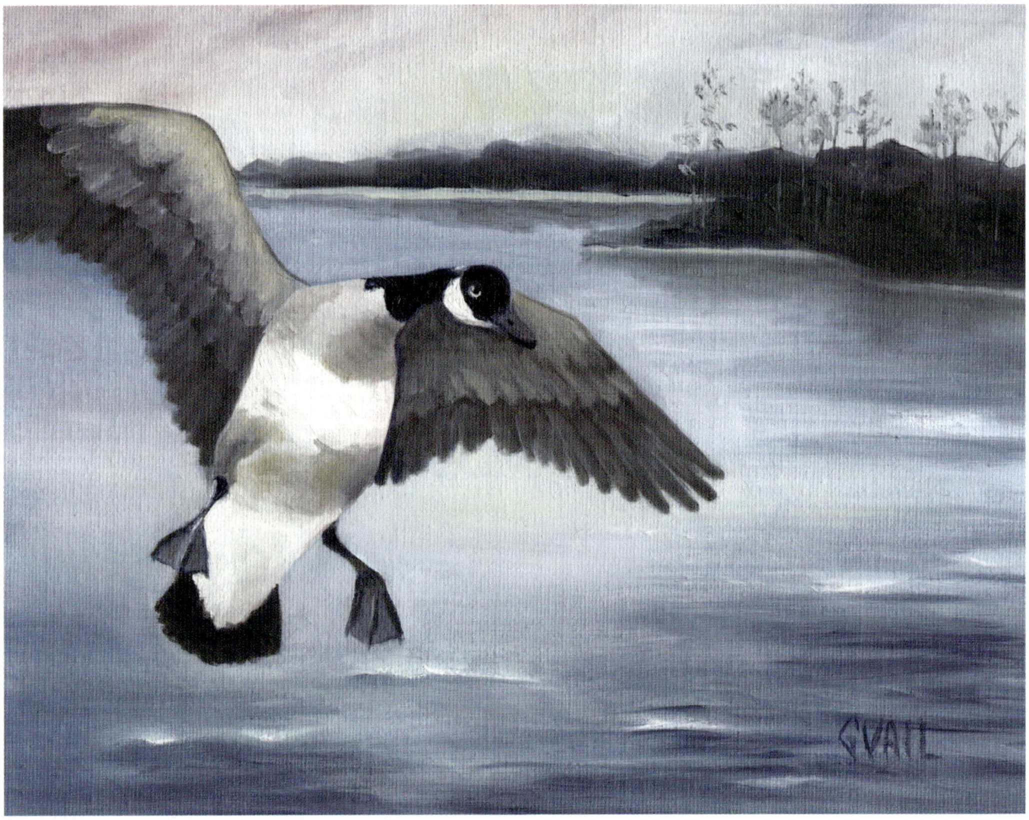

Gail Vail, Oil

The Urge to Fly

A dozen geese stayed to winter
on our frozen lake while
their flock spread great wings
to sail on chilling currents south.

Those left behind paraded
in the snow, stretching banded
necks until honking of their clan
whispered into gray.

Decision moment gone, they freed
an edge of lake from ice and dined
on remnant corn. Their kingdom
small, their comfort cold,

their choice was told with trumpets.
The urge to fly is in all blood.
Staying is the gravity that grips
both cowardly and brave.

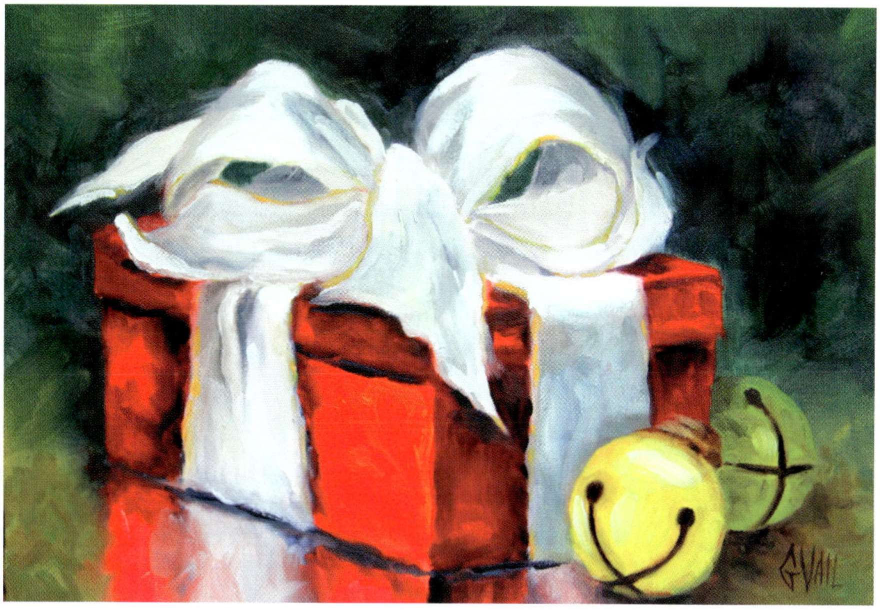

Gail Vail, Oil

The Gift

By late October, the Queen mother of our family had become a frail figure tightly confined by hospital sheets. A forest of stainless steel trees surrounded her bed, their curved limbs hung with surging pumps and gauges that measured her medications with clicks relentless as clocks beating out the end of time. On the black screen above her, my mother's ninety-six years were reduced to five darting green lines.

Doctors gave us their advice. She had congestive heart failure and at her age, her odds were long, our options few. Even so, we made the decision hesitantly. During the night, oxygen from the ventilator would gradually decrease and she would need to breathe on her own. Her fate rested on a tired heart and that inborn gallantry that honors all sorts of battlefields… "the will to live."

The night passed in jagged hours. We took turns at her bedside. My wife stroked her hands. I sang the old hymns she favored. Twice each hour, angels came into the darkened room. Without benefit of wings, they circled the fluorescent landscape, bestowing practiced grace. A needle of relief. A touch of a hand. Reassuring words whispered to a distant mind. The gentle work of white-starched seraphim.

Finally, the ventilator stopped giving breath and she began to flail against the dying light. The seismograph of her heart dipped and rose erratically. Then her restless soul soared to the edge of the universe. It circled faint, exploding stars born long before time itself. Finally, it drifted slowly back toward earth until the patterns on the screen became familiar. She was breathing on her own.

In the weeks following her hospitalization my mother accepted hugs from her three grandchildren. She felt the arms of seven great grandchildren encircle her neck. The laughing company of friends and neighbors brightened long hours of convalescence. Her strength returned gradually, buoyed by the ebb and flow of kindnesses and compassion surrounding her.

In December we wrapped gifts with curling bows and laid them under splendid trees. But the most precious gift was already ours---the elusive, fragile, miraculous gift of a loved one's life.

It is the same gift celebrated when a perfect child was born in a stable, amid startled sheep and anxious shepherds two thousand years ago. And now it is the grant of a long life sustained a bit longer. These are Christmas gifts that know no season, those received throughout the world every second of every day. They are worthy of celebration. They are also worthy of prayer.

Christmas Eve: The Fine Print

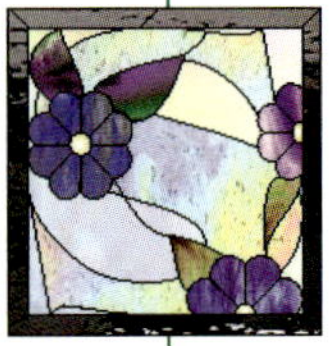

ome assembly is required," it states coyly on the box,
a devious understatement of the battle still ahead,
a fib that grows colossal as sweat flows down my cheek,
a perjury more deceitful as my cheeks are turning red.

Christmas Eve draws to a close. There is peace at last.
Stockings are all hung and filled. Kids are fast asleep.
My wife tiptoes past me on her way to slumber land
while I toil to build a toy from pieces in a heap.

I'm in the second hour of my "some assembly" task,
contents of my toolbox scattered round me on the floor.
Instructions writ in foreign lands create a mental fog.
"Connect A to Z then to Four" does not clarify my chore.

The action toy looked simple when I saw it on display.
An elderly saleslady claimed assembly by herself.
"It took me just ten minutes, and mechanical I'm not!
But pay another twenty and take this one off the shelf."

Pay twenty extra dollars for a pre-assembled toy?
It's now after midnight and I'd give her thirty five!
My kids soon will discover me as sun is coming up
whimpering and bleary eyed and narrowly alive.

Wait! Now I've found a web site with engineering tips.
The project is progressing. The end may be in sight.
The clock is striking two, just three pieces more to fit.
Looks like the picture on the box. I must have it right.

It's finally time to test this toy, see how it performs.
But my action toy lacks action. Now I have concluded
the power problem lies with my own brainpower supply.
I missed the fine print on the box "batteries not included."

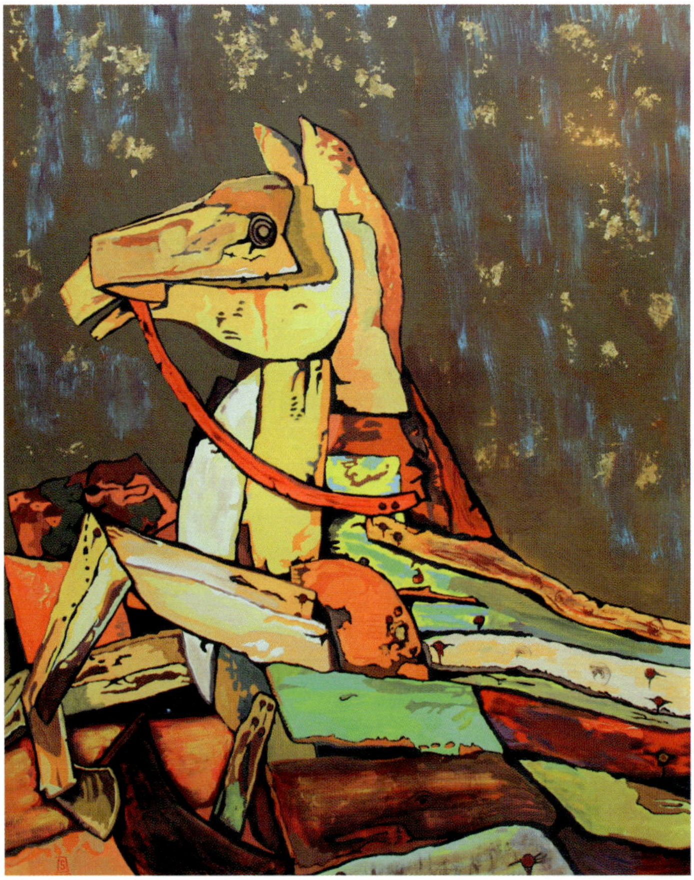

David Siffert, Gouache

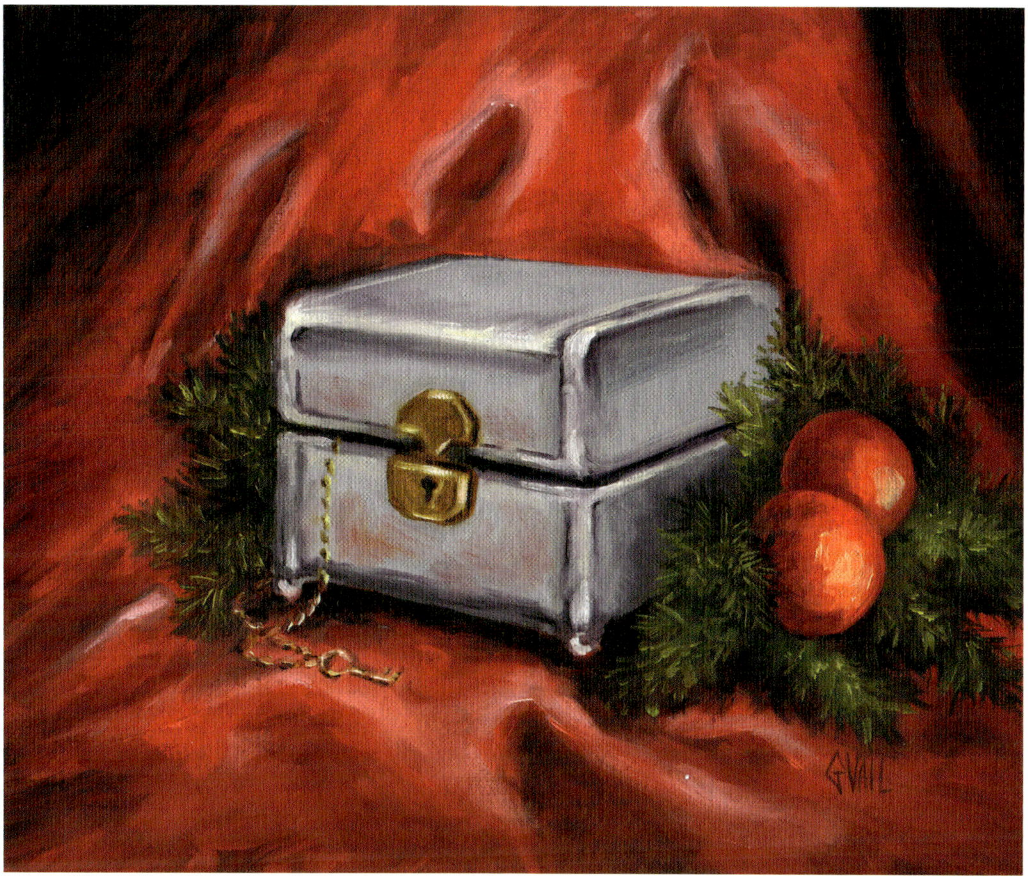

Gail Vail, Oil

The Polished Box

A lifetime of notes written in my mind
are locked within a polished box.
They lay upon each other as incidental
lovers, touching without feeling.

Glorious moments, lesser moods,
trapped in scraps of time like autumn
leaves pressed within a book. Kindling
cut for fires now long dark.

A treasury of faces I once loved,
names shamelessly forgotten.
My wealth of diamonds and rust
kept in dark custody, securely stored

until a page of memory is turned
and sunlight flickers on a blue pearl sea.
Until night rain slides down a window,
slowly, as a woman combs her hair.

Until a melody I'd left behind
suspends the beating of my heart.
Then ghosts come pleading for the key.
The polished box flings open,

time and place are rearranged.
Years peel away. Memories come
heartache quick. Hard-cut diamonds
surround me in a glittering swirl.

I am then the poorest of the rich.
I am then the richest of the poor.

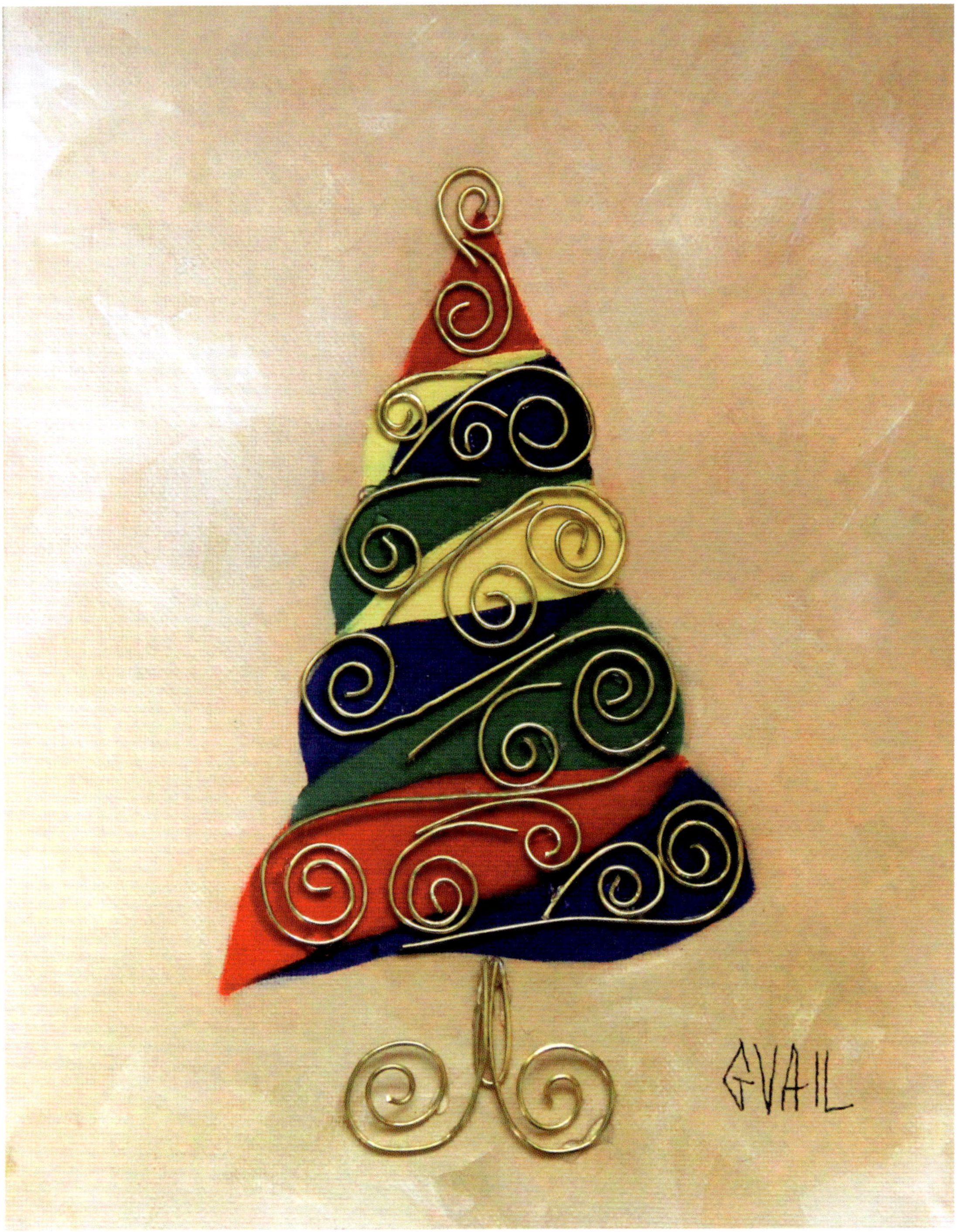

Gail Vail, Mixed Media

Hospice

The light from the hall left its white imprint
on the vinyl floor. Deeper in the shadows
of the room, a man of ninety two struggled
to swing his feet off the edge of the bed.
The young nurse in the chair beside him rose
to lay a gentle restraining hand on his arm
and he slumped back against his pillow.

"Where do you want to go, Ed?" she asked quietly.

"Need to get to Michigan," he said, propping
himself on his elbows. "Goin' up for Christmas.
Better get movin'. Don't wanna be late.
Stuff is all packed. Should I take my pills?"

"I don't think you'll need them,"she said.
"But how about a sweater? Will you be cold?"

"There'll be snow," he said. "Always snows
at Christmastime. But never seems cold to me."

"Michigan sounds nice," she said. "Peaceful.
A good place to be for Christmas."

"Shirley's already there," he said. "She'll be makin'
fudge and pumpkin bread. Always fixes a big meal.
Suppose the kids'll be late. Always are."

"You'll have time to yourselves, then," she said.
"Just the two of you before your family comes."

"Yeah, that'll be nice" he said. He relaxed into
the pillow and closed his eyes. "We can make a fire
and talk about times we had. Be good to see her,"
he said, the words now coming soft and slow.
"Since she's been gone I miss her every day."

"I know you do,"she said, "but it won't be long
before you're together again." She squeezed his hand.
"I just want you to know that I'll miss you, too.
You'll have a wonderful Christmas...up in Michigan."

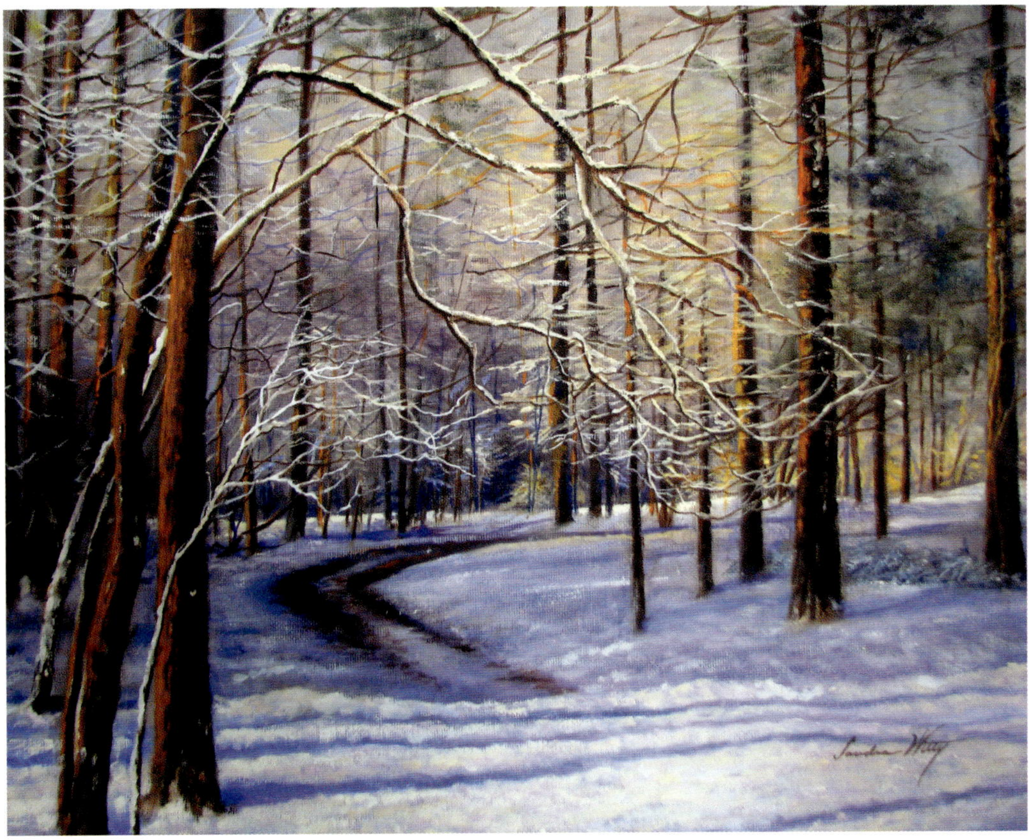

Sandra Witty, Oil

The Rise and Fall of the Southern Snowman

In central Georgia, a forecast of snow provokes the same sort of anxiety the area experienced in 1864 when Union General "Uncle Billy" Sherman made his decision to march to the sea on local roads. In both cases, something unnatural of northern origin is on its way. Genteel life amid the tall pines and sprouting crocuses is in for a drastic change.

Adult Georgians welcome snow as they might a tsunami or volcanic eruption. Since fleeing the coming storm on potentially icy roads would indicate a degree of lunacy reserved for Tennessee or Florida football fans, everyone in the path of the storm simply goes into hiding. Before the first flake touches red dirt, notices of closings crawl across the television screen throughout the evening news and into American Idol. There will be no PTA meetings. No Elks. No AA. No high school basketball. Chicken and dumpling dinners hosted by Baptist ladies are canceled. To underscore the severity of the situation, TV weathermen…or, more correctly, weatherpersons …don earmuffs and scarves as they plot the white mass marching menacingly toward Atlanta.

Last year my wife was shopping in Macon when an announcement boomed over speakers. "Due to the severe weather, the mall will be closing at 4p.m." Since she had an hour drive home, she asked a security guard when the severe weather was expected. "About noon tomorrow," he told her solemnly.

While adult Georgians shy from snow as if it were poison gas, the younger populace can't wait for the skies to open up and front lawns to be blanketed in white. Where Southern kids are concerned, snow is a life changing substance. Schools close and stay closed until the yellow buses can navigate their routes safely. Since snow plows in these parts are rarer than liberal politicians, that can take several days. In the meantime, there is fun awaitin' on Georgia hills, especially if a cobweb-covered sled is still hanging in the garage. If not, a garbage can lid will suffice. College students have been known to speed down slopes on plastic trays liberated from their cafeteria.

With parents unable to get to work or go to book club and kids excused from school, the unexpected togetherness soon wears thin. Offspring are urged to stay outdoors and enjoy the rare excitement that snow offers. They are allowed back inside only when tinged with blue.

It is at this meteorological juncture that we experience the rise of the southern snowman. To begin, some basic knowledge is required. First, Dixie snow has a much shorter lifespan than Yankee snow. Its evolution into mush begins within a day or so. Picturesque white beards added to the genial faces of pansies will disappear overnight. So photographers need to move quickly to capture muffin topped mailboxes and white laced gingerbread porches. The upside is that wet snow makes great snowballs. And really great snowmen.

Snowmen…alright, I suppose political correctness applies here, too…snowpersons are traditionally engineered by first compacting a wad of snow into the size and shape of a softball. As that embryo is rolled and pushed across the lawn, it usually grows to the height of a pick-up tire. That serves as the lower torso. The process is repeated… with time out for hot chocolate…until the next two balls of snow are heaved into place to create the upper torso and head. Rolling this frozen anatomy exposes paths of grass sprouting on the lawn. So a true Georgia snowman is artfully centered in a starburst of green. That starburst is a welcome sign that mother nature will return to her warmer ladylike form shortly. It should be noted that Yankee snowmen never see green grass. No starburst. Nothing to indicate there are warm times ahead. Yankee snowmen live longer but have emotional problems.

Once the heavy lifting is over, the real fun starts. Budding artists start giving their creation a personality. Noses are added made of carrots, zucchini or toilet paper rolls. Eyes are surgically embedded, some made of tennis balls or paper cups sketched with wild magic marker expressions. A mouth is fashioned with yarn, salvaged golf balls, or, in rural areas, rows of unshelled pecans. Pecans, however, tend to look as if severe tooth decay has set in.

Fashion accessories selected for snowpeople depends largely on property owners loyalties. Red hats, badges, scarves promoting the Georgia Bulldogs are common. Georgia Tech and local school paraphernalia are also favored. Unlike the corn-cob smoking "Frosty" made famous in song, snowmen in these parts are entirely tobacco free.

To portray a solid work ethic, tools such as a rakes or shovels are propped against a snowman's torso. Patriotic snowmen proudly hold flags and wear American Legion caps. Sporting snowmen carry golf bags and hold old wooden drivers in their icy grip. Designer conscious households attire their snowperson in dresses and shawls rescued from the going-to-the-Goodwill bag. A straw hat with brightly colored band often completes the ensemble.

Since Dixie snowpersons have a short life, it doesn't take long before their robust figures undergo rapid weight loss and the art and appliances fixed to them begin to slide. One snowman was ingeniously decked out with political posters, buttons and cap favoring a local candidate. Then there was a quick thaw. The opposition took a picture of him suffering collapse with a particularly unsightly sag of nose and mouth. It became an election ad in the local paper, and probably caused snowmen to permanently retire from politics.

Even so, the last, mushy moments of a southern snowman's life offer a symbolic, hopeful message, evidence that snow has come and gone from central Georgia. Roads are clear. The mall is open. School buses are rolling. The rusty sled that relived a day or two of former glory is once more hanging in the garage. Pansies are still smiling and spring is on the way.

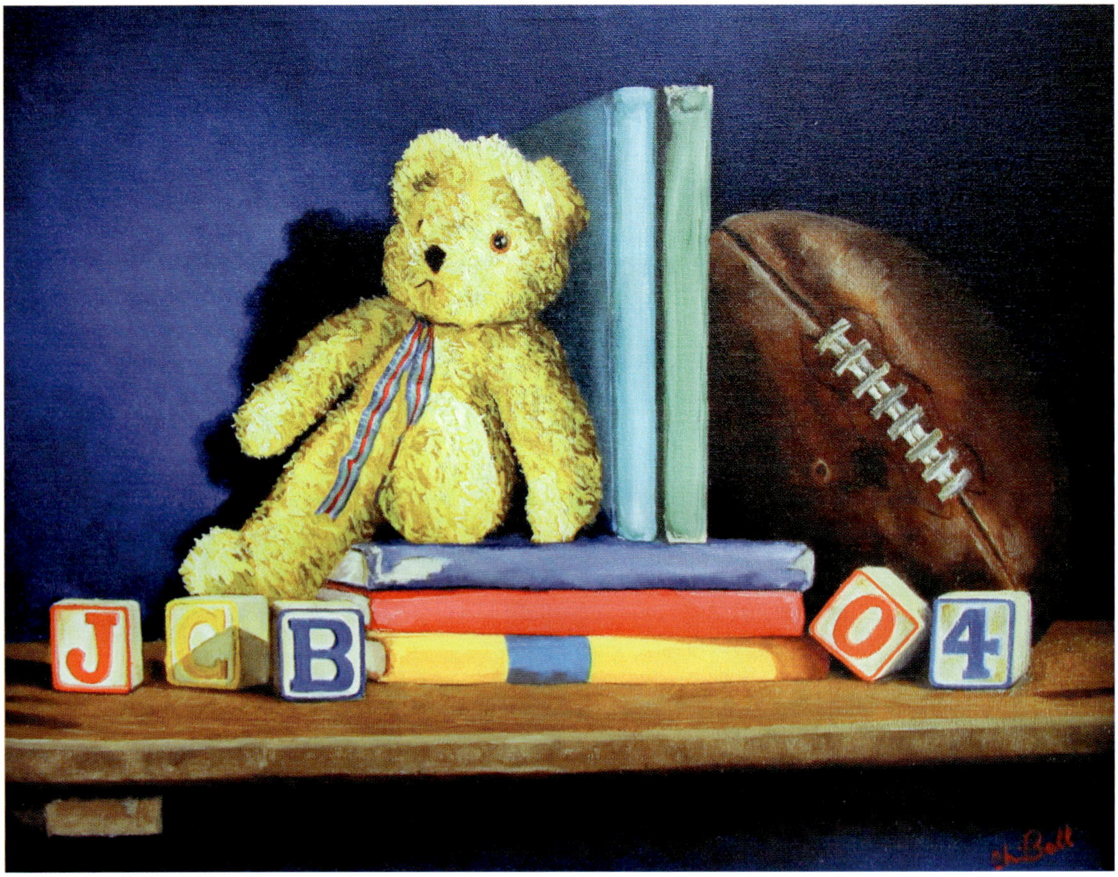

Chris Ball, Oil

Evolution

I.

A sliver of memory brings
the feel of cool, polished steel,
a fighter airplane discovered
under tinseled spruce one
Christmas morning a lifetime ago.
A gift of my dreams my parents
could not easily afford, mine to
hold aloft, to climb and dive.
I hugged my Mom and Dad
until they gave in to laughter.
"It's just what I wanted."

II.

A carol was sung by shivering
schoolboys, a melody to comfort
old and ill confined to a house
in need of paint and hope.
From the edge of the porch
we sang as pale faces peered
through frost laced windows.
We framed the door cautiously
as their eyes consumed us.
"Joy To The World" we caroled,
"the Lord is come." Then we ran,
without knowing why, into
the comfort of the night.

III.

The antiseptic smell infecting
the air of the children's ward
was lightened that day with
peppermint and pine.
I was the party's naïve Santa,
recruited from a nearby school,
a Santa unprepared for the
shortfall in his pack, the lack of
redeeming toys for kids without
normal gifts of sight and sound
or average life expectancy.
A girl of five with hazel eyes and
clean shaved head smiled shyly
as I carelessly handed her a doll
with long and flowing curls.
Suddenly, my nylon beard
could not absorb my tears.
"Merry Christmas" was the
only prayer I could conceive.
Then she said with soft affection
"I love you, Santa," and it was
all I wanted to hear.

IV.

Two days after Christmas
I tied four blue balloons
to our mailbox by the road.
The wind was sharp, my
fingers numbed before the
knots were fast.
A fifth balloon was left
to skate on winter wind,
skim the ice glazed snow,
sail above a jagged line
of shadowed trees.
I hoped it would fly north
where our new grandchild
slept, exhausted by new life.
It chose, instead, to dance
in silent celebration
then drift straight into
the blue pool of moon.
I spoke aloud to the sky
that claimed it. "Thanks,
he is just what we wanted."

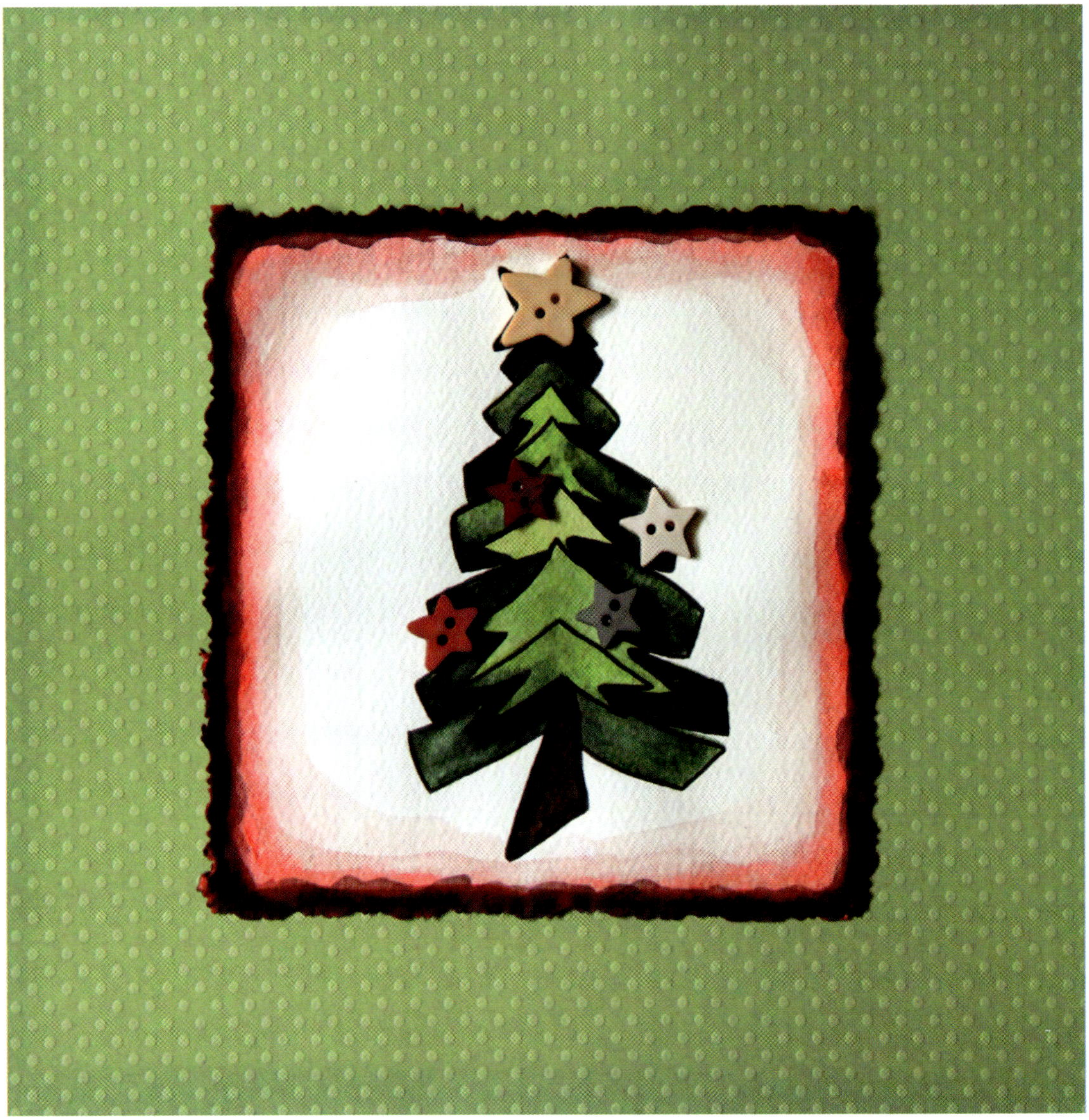

Gail Vail, Mixed Media

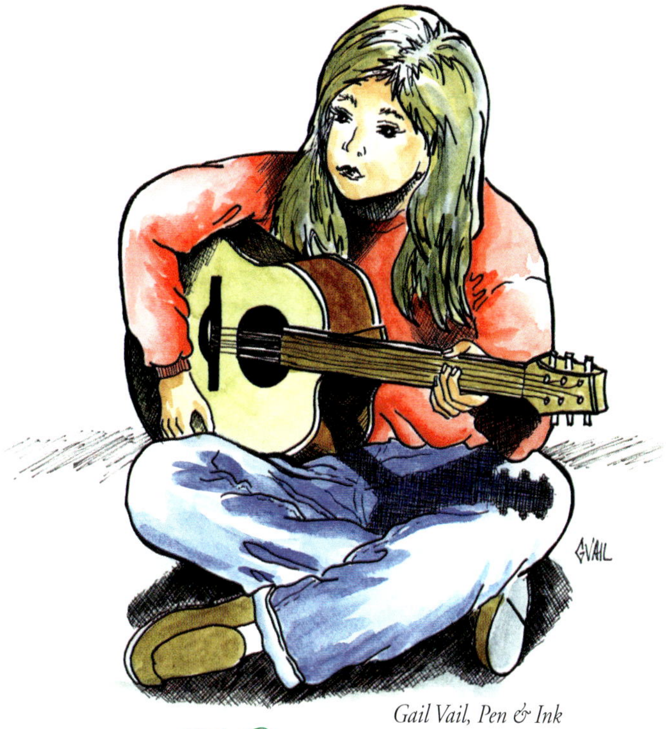

Gail Vail, Pen & Ink

Homecoming

On Christmas Eve a blizzard crushed the hopes of holiday travelers waiting at the airport and stranded gift-wrapped cargo intended for tomorrow. Jet engines whined to a stop. Snowplows surrendered the runways to the storm and sat passively on ramps, their whirling red lamps fading behind a curtain of white.

Gates soon overflowed. All of the chairs and most of the floor spaces were occupied. A soldier in desert camouflage and polished boots stood to offer his seat to a mother balancing her travel bag and a cranky two-year old. Then he moved through the crowd and leaned his forehead wearily against the window watching snow swirl around baggage wagons and pile up on silver wings.

On the floor next to him, a girl of college age was propped against her backpack. For a moment she absorbed his quiet sadness. Then she asked tentatively, "Comin' from Iraq?"

"No, missed that one," the soldier said. "I pulled duty in Afghanistan. First time I've been home in over a year." A gust rattled the window. "Make that almost home." His smile didn't mask his disappointment.

The girl's dark hair spilled over her knees as she extracted a guitar from a case quilted with travel stickers. She tuned it and strummed chords that drifted unnoticed into the pool of restlessness around her. "Don't worry soldier. Rudolph will get you through," she grinned confidently. Then she sang of that rescuing reindeer in clear, sweet tremolo. After that, she sang of jingle bells, four calling birds and the first noel. Gradually, conversations throughout the gate area grew faint until only the girl's voice hung in the air like a silver strand.

As she played "Silent Night" tentative voices joined hers in recollected harmonies that rolled down the marble corridors. Travelers at other gates stopped to listen. Soon almost everyone was singing, bonded in a ceremony of ancient carols. "Oh Little Town Of Bethlehem" they sang. In the neon canyons of the crowded terminal, Christmas Eve finally passed unnoticed into Christmas morning.

By now the soldier was sitting next to the longhaired girl, adding his rasping voice to hers. They were a comfortable pair of pilgrims in the company of waylaid travelers who found shelter from the howling storm in songs and memories. The young soldier's journey had been long, but he had found the place he was looking for. Tomorrow he still had miles to go. Tonight he had come home.

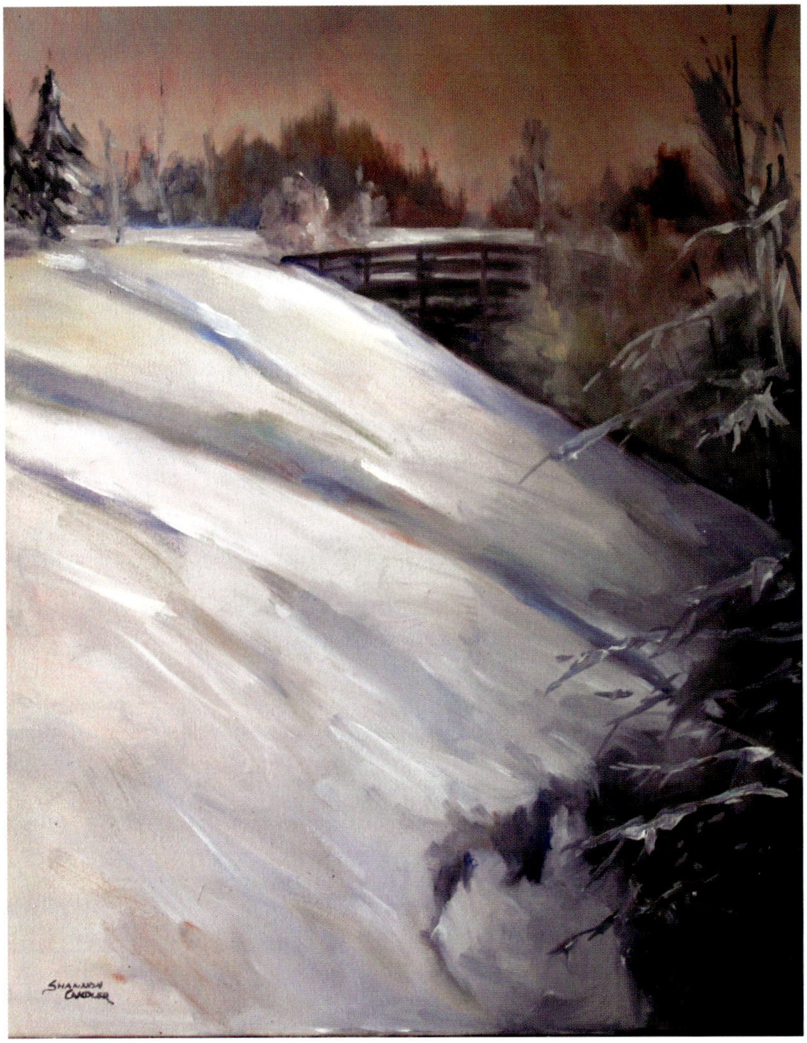

Shannon Candler, Oil

Snowbound in the Mountains of Heaven

My grandparents lived on an Iowa acreage 15 miles from my boyhood home. Their hilltop was my Himalayan kingdom. Fred and Gladder owned the real estate. But the spirits in this exotic kingdom were mine to exorcise, its mysteries mine to explore.

By July woods bordering their yard were thick and smelled of sweet decay. In their dark ravines I heard drums of death and saw stalking shadows. From atop a boulder Fred assured me was a meteorite, I could see the silvered River of No Return.

As autumn moved toward winter, oaks and elms gave up their leaves and distances came pouring through. Standing on the meteorite, I could see gilded pagodas of Kathmandu. In the blue haze beyond them lay white-tipped Mountains of Heaven.

When I was nine, I came to the hill early for Christmas. As Dad's Dodge pulled away, it began to snow. The day vanished under broad, white strokes. That night I lay in an attic bed under quilts Gladys made, and felt the storm pound on the roof Fred built.

Next morning drifts leaned against the door, yard and bushes entombed in white. The power was out. No traffic moved. "I guess we're snowbound," Gladder said as if she had expected it all along. Yes, snowbound in the Mountains of Heaven.

Over breakfast, Fred spun out tales of blizzards he survived as a railroad brakeman, rapping his pipe on the chair as the action got hot. Gladder quietly peeled apples. "What was the worst storm for you?" I asked her. "Oh," she smiled, "probably this one."

Next day the road was plowed, and Fred and I shoveled out the drive. Early Christmas Eve the family Dodge brought Mom and Dad, groceries and gifts. Then other wheel-spinning sedans braved the hill, and a dozen relatives and hot dishes were assembled.

Gifts were exchanged in the glow of kerosene lamps and favorite Christmases were called to mind. "What was yours, Gladys?" I asked. She looked about at those who had made the hard journey to the snowbound Mountains of Heaven "Oh, I think---this one."

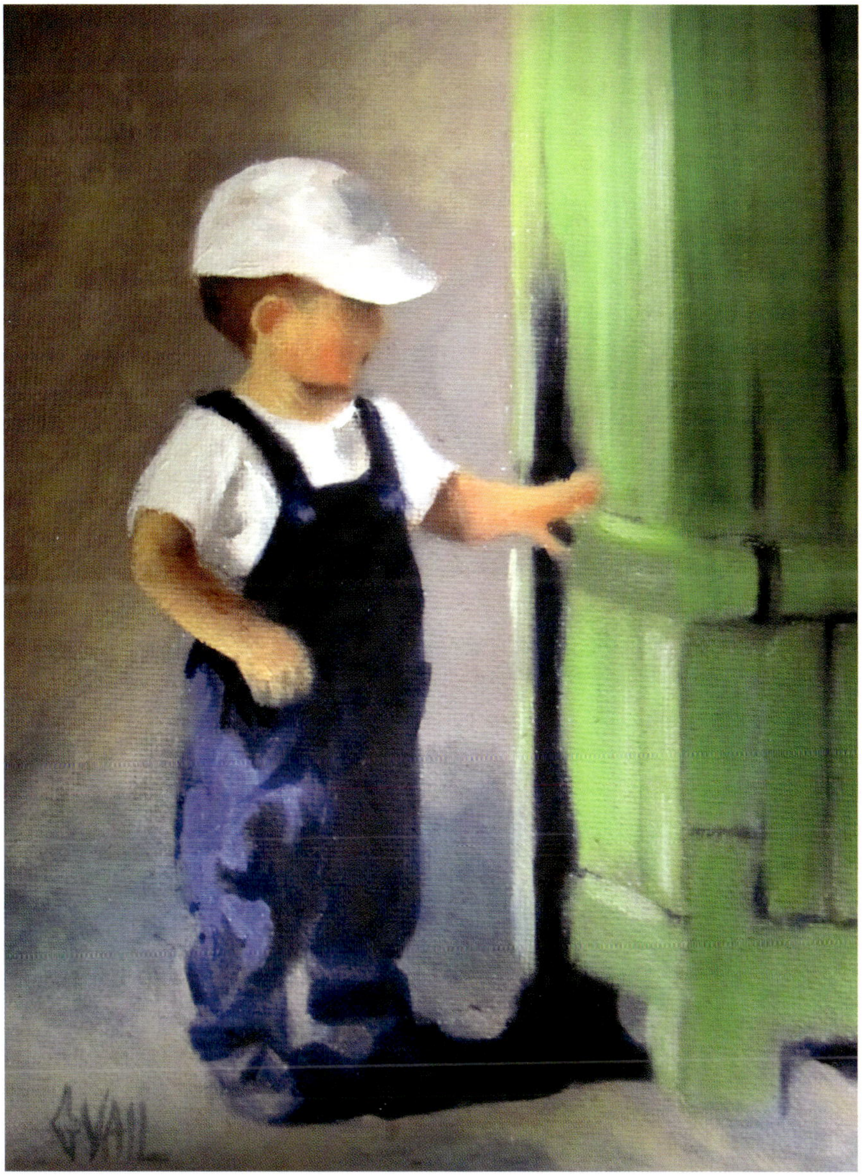

Gail Vail, Oil

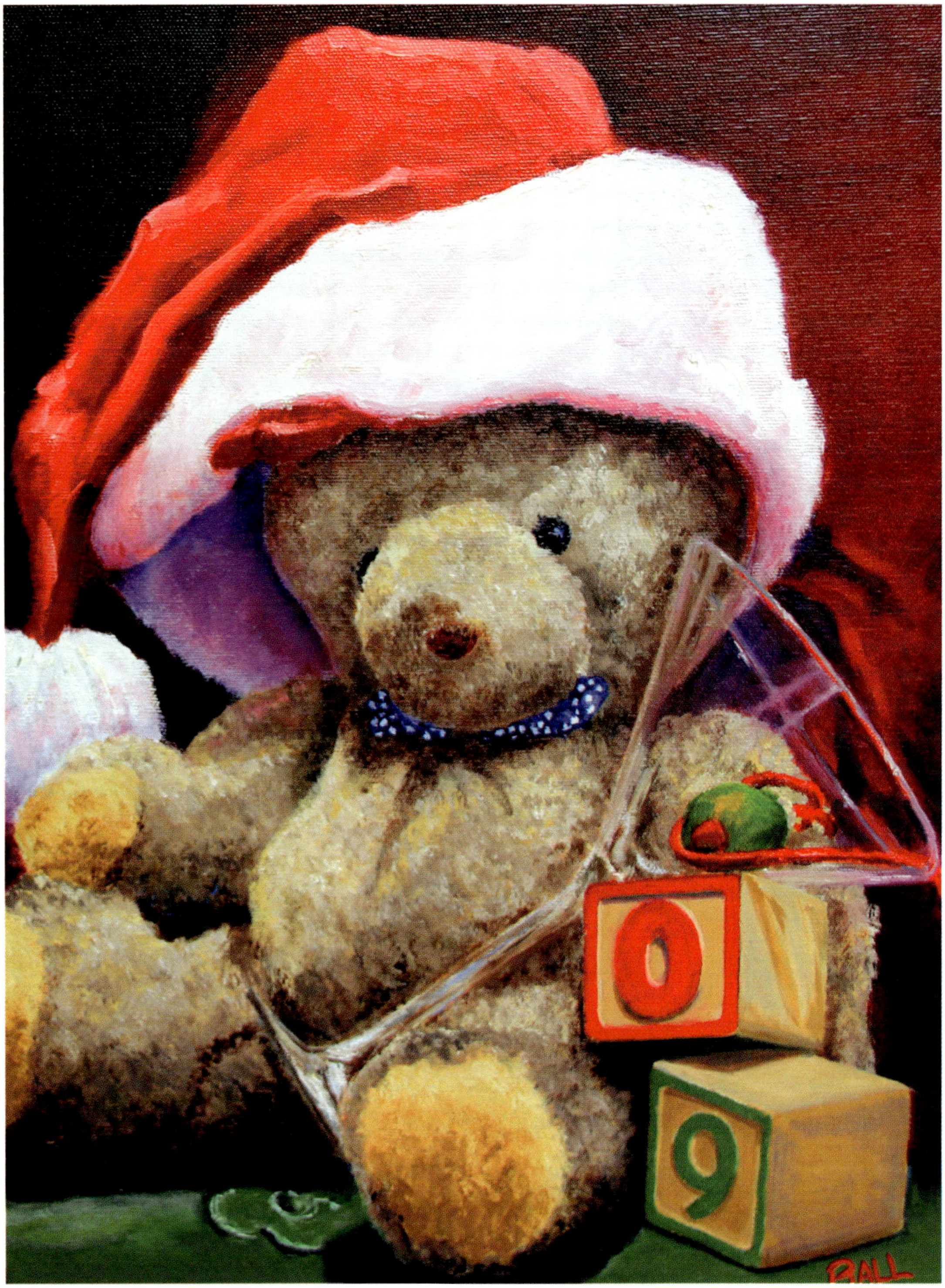

Chris Ball, Oil

Filling Spaces

It is the afternoon of Christmas Eve. A parent-enforced armistice has brought temporary peace to our son's home in Minnesota. A hand-printed note flutters down from the hallway on the second floor. It is from seven-year-old-and-trying-to-be-patient grandson Drew. "Is quiet time over yet?" it inquires plaintively. Mercifully, it is and the holiday din of a five-family houseful resumes.

When the curtain finally goes up on Christmas Eve, the stage is set with Dickens-like images. There is a giant tree in a spacious room bordered with colored lights and a wassail feast with ample wine. Aunt Lisa plays the organ and we respond with lyrics of carols etched in our memories. Two cousins offer an impromptu recital on violin and viola. Then seven-year-old Drew climbs atop a piano stool and sings "Silent Night" in a voice clear and sustaining as winter stars. Not one to be theatrically outdone, his younger sister Ali follows with "Santa Claus Is Coming To Town," wagging an accusing finger to warn us "You'd better not pout." But tonight no one is pouting.

By ten o'clock next morning, lists hand-printed in crayon a month earlier have been fulfilled and painstakingly wrapped boxes have been reduced to rubble. Stephanie is wearing her new blue and white Timberwolves jersey. It drapes to her ankles and displays the number three, her age. A white bow is stuck on her bottom designating her as official dispenser of adult gifts, and she is dispensing them in a ring-announcer's voice. "This present's for DONNA!"

Eight-month-old twins have been cuddled and passed about and have come to rest on the lap of their aunt, safe above the plunging surf of paper and buzzing toys. Harrison looks quietly bewildered. Hannah's eyes are big blue buttons of wonder, her copper hair shocked into a kewpie-curl. Her legs and arms pump frantically. The Ghost of Christmas Yet To Come, it would seem, is dancing toward her across the toy-strewn floor.

Cameron, age two, stands alone at the window watching large flakes descend languidly from the gray sky. "It nosing," he observes helpfully. Sure enough, our white Christmas is being replenished, and there is a momentary pause as we watch the snow fall.

In that silence, we feel an empty space in the room and in our hearts. The great grandmother who has always reigned over our Christmas mornings is not here. Great Grandma Flossie is gone and each of us feels her loss deeply, even though we can't bring ourselves to speak of it. Her luminescent smile encircled every one of our family celebrations like a string of pearls. But as we glance around the chattering room, we are blessed with the discovery that it still surrounds us. Flossie's smile and twinkling eyes have been miraculously transferred to smaller faces. In the next moment, her great grandchildren erupt in laughter and the silence is broken. The space in our heart seems full again.

Perhaps, on second thought, it was never really empty.

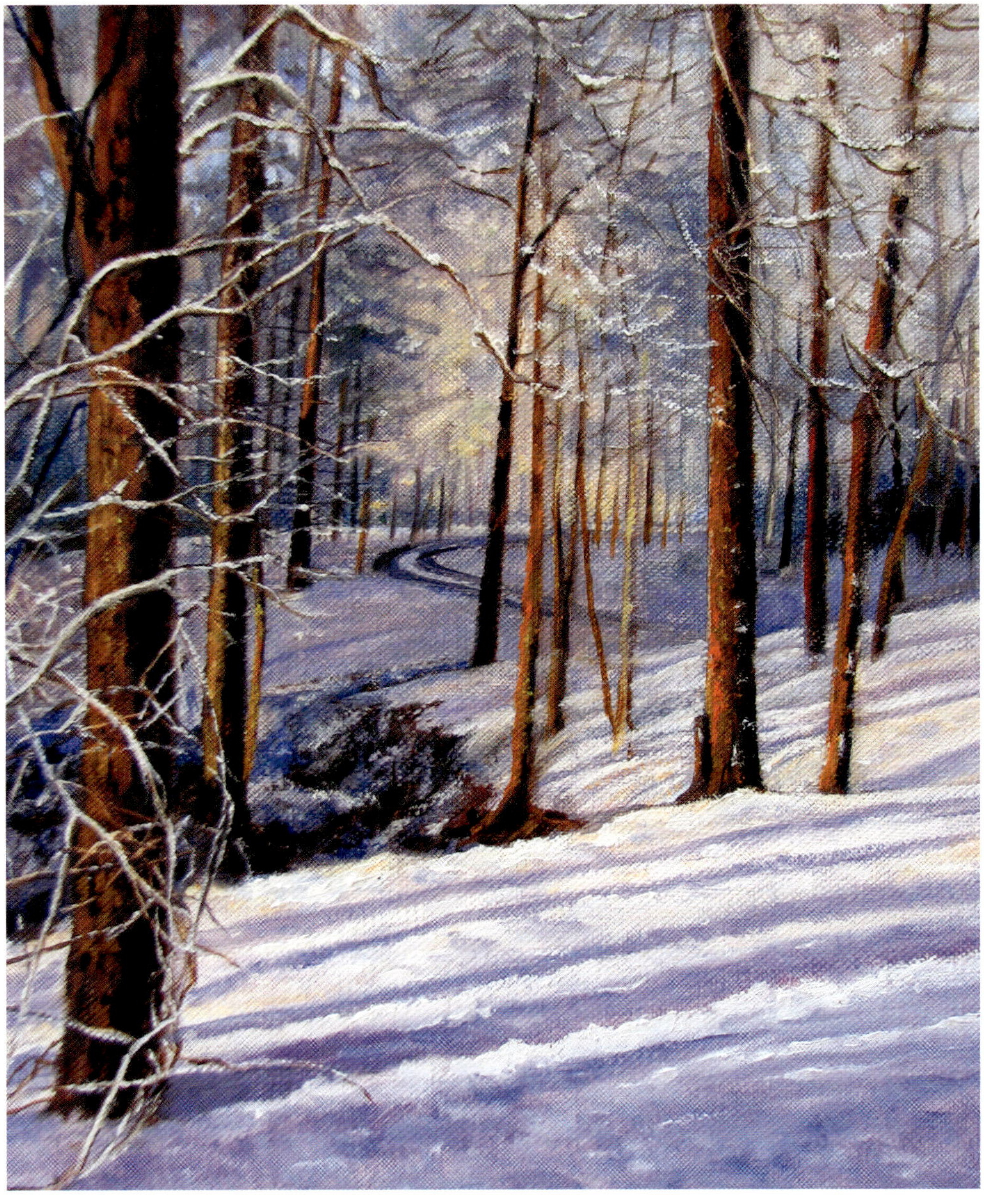

Sandra Witty, Oil

Blizzard Grits

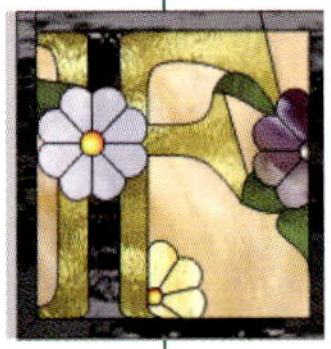rom: danieljholcum@gmail.com
Sent: Tuesday, February 1, 2011 9:50 PM
To: janetc@taratary.net
Subject: Report from Up North

Bad news, Janci. I'm not goin' to make it to Milledgeville for the social at Kappa Delta on Valentine's Day. I'm really down about it 'cause I was lookin' for some closeup time with you. Problem is, my finances are flatter than a Huddle House pancake.

Life here in Minneapolis has been really grim of late. When I was asked to turn in my orange apron at the Home Stuff store, I figured I could swing another floor job at a competitor. Fat chance! Turns out big box managers are cozy as fleas on a coon hound. Your sweet-talkin' Georgia boy is on a "don't hire" list that's flying around the Twin Cities like a turkey vulture. And what was my big crime? I gave a straight answer to a customer's question about a barbecue grill we featured! I told him "Sir, I wouldn't use that thing to grill road kill." Now I ask, wasn't that being helpful? My boss didn't think so. He pulls me over and suggests I rephrase--or else! So I go back to the customer and say, "Sir, I was maybe too negative about this unit. I guess I *would* use it to grill road kill." Well, that did it! Bosses up here just do not value southern sincerity.

But as daddy used to say, "sicker dogs than this got well." Here's some good news. I got a temporary job. My cousin Ellen and her husband Richard are goin' to Paris and she asked if I could stay at their house in Minnetonka and look after things for two weeks. They've got two kids in high school, Alan a senior, and Steph a junior. No diapers to change or Gerber's to spoon. Ellen and Richard took one car to the airport and left us a 4-wheel SUV to come and go in the snow of which there is likely to be a lot. Most of my time will be spent walkin' the dog and makin' sure the kids don't send out party invitations to the whole school on Facebook. Will let you know when I'm settled in. Loveya, home skillet. DJ.

Sent: Thursday, February 10, 2011 11;25 AM
To: janetc@taratary.net
Subject: Way Too Much White

Janci, darlin', great to get your note. Sorry to hear you already spent a ton on new threads for the dance. Since I left you hangin', I can't groan about your asking Harris Mathews to escort you, even though I think he's a real frat brat. I won't be there to play defense, so my advice is stick close to your sorority mom that night. That boy's got faster hands than a major league shortstop.

This MN weather is killin' all my GA genes. In January there was heat wave when the temp got up to 20 degrees with only six inches of snow on the ground. Then three days ago---as soon as Ellen and Richard took off---it started comin' down. Now we've got two and a half feet on the ground and it's not lettin' up! I'm goin' snow blind. Bad enough it's totally white outside, but like, even the FOOD we eat is white. Last night we warmed up mashed potatoes and Swedish meatballs Ellen stashed away for us. If there had been BBQ sauce on the meatballs, I could have found them a lot easier.

Whenever its time to take the dog out another storm blows in. Belle is a sweet pup, but guess what color she is? Totally white. When I walk her in a blizzard it looks like I'm pulling an empty leash.

Hate to say it, darlin', but my luck is still goin' south even though I'm not. When I got up this mornin', the temp in the house was 50. Alan and Steph were brought up in this climate so they hardly noticed. Boy I did! I put on my Georgia College jacket and a muffler and called the furnace guy. So he says, "I'll come out tomorrow if the power stays on, which could be a problem with the storm that's comin' our way."

I'm askin' myself, why doesn't everybody up here, like, live in an igloo and totally forget about central heating? Anyway, we decided it was better if the kids stayed with friends until the heat comes back on. Steph caught a ride to ski practice and Alan drove to basketball practice. So this morning it's just Belle and me buried under quilts, puffing white clouds and watchin' the family room windows frost over.

I cooked myself some grits and eggs for lunch and they tasted like home until I opened the door to let Belle out to do her business. I'm standin' with the grits in my hand when a clump of snow comes off the roof and dropped smack dab in the bowl. That leaves me with blizzard grits and ten frozen toes which I 'm coaxin' the dog to lay on.

Since you're a steady church goer, Janci, please pray the furnace man shows tomorrow.

Sent: Friday, February 11, 2011 12;07 PM
To: janetc@taratary.net
Subject: Blower motors and ski sprains

Your prayer worked, Janci! The furnace guy---old dude named Gunderson---shows up this morning after stompin' through the three foot drifts on the front walk. He goes down and pats the furnace like it was a Kentucky thoroughbred and says, "needs a new blower motor and fly wheel. Won't take long to install--unless they's on back order. I can call an' check now—except can't usually get clear cell reception out here. Could use your landline—if it's still workin'. Lot's of lines down last night."

Like, this dude seems almost disappointed when he finds his phone works and the parts are in. To overcome all that good news, he goes on to tell me about the disaster we barely ducked. " Lucky that blower didn't blow up on ya. Doesn't happen often," then he adds, "- but it could! Anyways, if it blew, it probably wouldn't catch fire - but seen it happen." So as he packs up, he says "I'll be back to install the motor tomorrow - unless the storm gets worse and the interstate shuts down." I guess Scandinavians don't naturally look on the bright side of things. Must be the lack of sunlight.

Just as Gunderson leaves, Steph shows up. On crutches. She tells me she twisted her knee at ski practice, but not to worry because the guy who brought her home is a doctor and has given her instructions on what to do, which is, she says, "take two Aleve, elevate my leg and apply cold to the swollen area. "I tell her applyin' cold is no problem---she can just hang out in the family room. Then I ask, "So this guy who brought you home, is he an orthopedic doc?" "No," she says, "he's a dentist."

Since I am in charge here and we are getting short on groceries, I will warm up some soup for dinner if Steph tells me where the pans are and how to work the stove and can opener. Up to now pizza has been, like, our basic food group since all the pizza delivery vans up here have 4-wheel drive. I guess I should do better at menu planning. Alan took the SUV, so if I can reach him , I'll see if he can pick up a bag of Hershey Mini's. You can see I'm turnin' into a real homemaker. Loveya sweet pea. DJ.

PS. Was real sorry to learn from you Harris Mathews got a new Mustang convertible.

Sent: Saturday, February 12 , 2011 10:40 PM
To: janetc@taratary.net
Subject: Steering clear of Viking food

Janci, really missed hearin' from you. Hope that's due to heavy class work and not because you're scootin' around in somebody's new ragtop.

Life in the Arctic is lookin' up, mostly because I'm learnin' how to delegate. Alan made it home last night bringing Chinese and a bag of Hershey's, and they were our best survival rations to date. He shoveled the steps and found wood dry enough to burn in the fireplace. Steph fixed soup for breakfast and was able to stand long enough to do the dishes. Good physical therapy, right?

It's still snowin' like crazy so we were couch jockeys today. No NASCAR on TV in these parts, so we watched a program on - you'll never believe this - guys fishing through holes in the ice. I needed two more blankets to finish it. I guess Gunderson is not an ice fisherman, since he shows up at three on a Saturday as promised . He has the blower motor and flywheel installed and the heat cranked up by four. When he comes up from the basement - you gotta love this old dude - he tells me "Boy, that's a load off. When them motors gives out, she's a real mess. Soot shootin' all over. Shouldn't be no problem now, though," he started to open the door to leave, then stopped "-unless yer heat exchanger up an' quits on ya. No tellin' bout that. Ya know, sometimes furnace innards just up an' give out together, like they caught some disease like bird flu or somethin'. Anyways, just give me a call if she goes an' I'll order up a new unit fer ya. Shouldn't take more than a week."

Then he opens the door and a blast of snow lifts the entry rug with Belle still lyin' on it. As the Gunderson walks away he says, "Course heat exchangers could be on back order. We're losing lots of 'em this winter." He is such a ray of sunshine.

Ellen and Richard called this afternoon. The kids lied like bootleggers and gave them a glowin' report. I told them about the furnace, but said household damage so far was minimal and the kids had not joined any gangs. They thought that was really funny, but it was late in Paris and they'd probably had a lot of wine.

Have an excellent time at the dance, Janci. But not TOO excellent. Missya, darlin', DJ.

Sent: Thursday, February 17, 2011 7:40 PM
To: janetc@taratary.net
Subject: Leaving Lapland

Janci, your email about the great time you had at the dance and how well you got on with Harris Mathews brought me down. WAY down! The idea of you dating that dorkus is hard to take while I'm stuck up here in Lapland. But I gotta tell you, your email made the bulb go on for me.

Janci, I'm leavin' MN and comin' back to GA where I belong. Ellen and Richard gave me a check for $800. That's enough to get me back to Milledgeville and put down a deposit at Georgia College for next semester. I'll list my major as Pre-Engineering. Who knows, I might end up in heating and air conditioning. Seems like a good future.

I should get to the Kappa Delta house sometime late Sunday, and I hope to see a yellow ribbon around the tree in front. I know my Ford pickup looks pretty sorry alongside a new Mustang. But if a Georgia boy is going to do serious dear hunting, a pickup is the preferred vehicle. And Janci, darlin', that's what I aim to do. Comin' atcha. DJ.

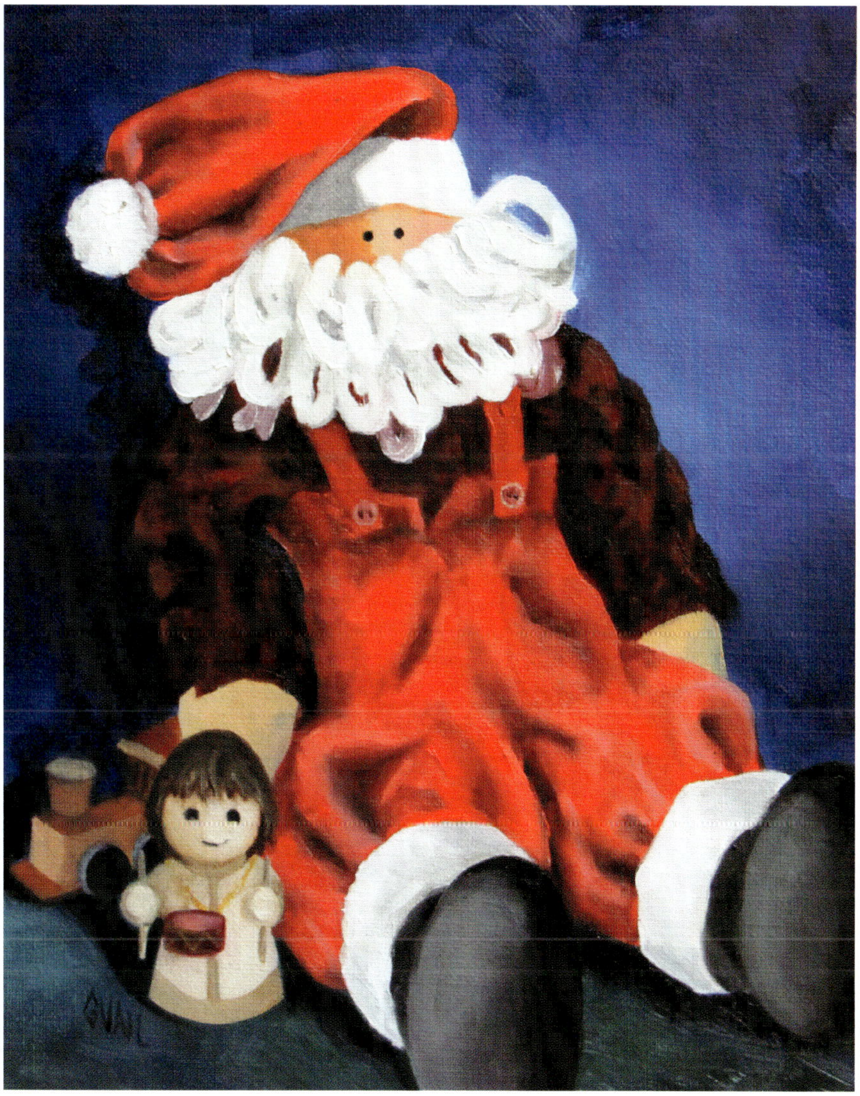

Gail Vail, Oil

AUTHOR & ARTIST

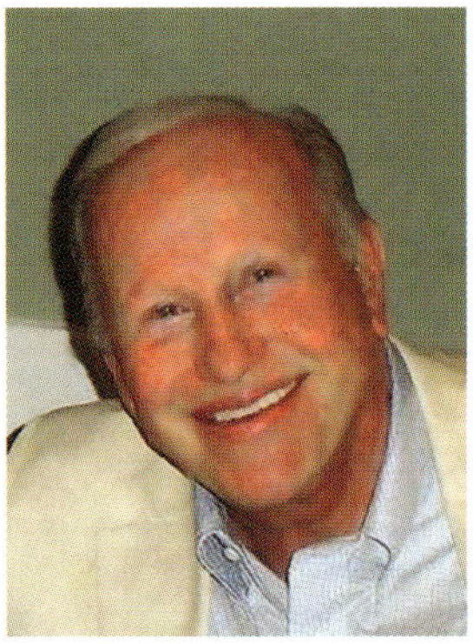

George Heiring

George Heiring is a master story teller whose work appears in national and regional publications. An Iowan by birth, he became a partner in a major international consulting firm headquartered near Chicago where he specialized in corporate communication. George and his wife Donna now live on Lake Oconee in central Georgia.

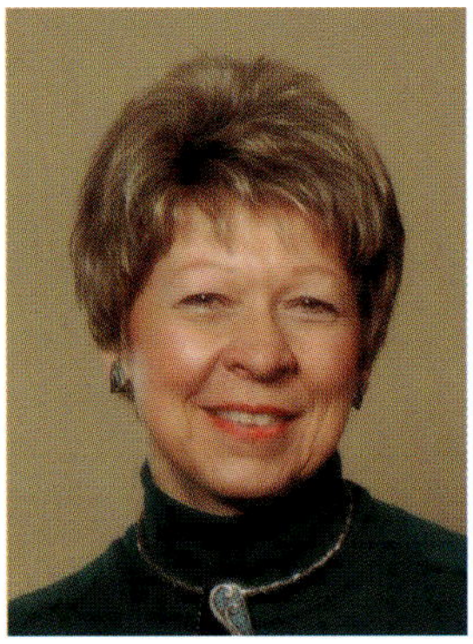

Gail Vail

Gail Vail has been an avid painter and writer for most of her life. Born in Nebraska, she earned a B.A. in Business and pursued a career in marketing and human resources with IBM. Gail and her husband Hugh are retired and live in Georgia's verdant lake country. She has again picked up her pen and her brush and is a co-owner of an art gallery.